Social Justice
and the
Christian Church

BY THE SAME WRITER

The Word of God and the Mind of Man

Freedom, Justice and the State

Ideas of History (editor)

The Light of the Mind: St. Augustine's Theory of Knowledge

The Philosophy of Gordon H. Clark (editor)

The Case for Biblical Christianity (editor)

The New Evangelicalism

Dooyeweerd and the Amsterdam Philosophy

Social Justice

and the

Christian Church

Ronald H. Nash
Western Kentucky University

MOTT
MEDIA

SOCIAL JUSTICE AND THE CHRISTIAN CHURCH

First Edition

Designed and edited by Leonard George Goss
Typeset by Joyce Bohn

Manufactured in the United States of America

ISBN 0-88062-008-0

Contents

    I. The Two Faces of Christian Social Concern   1

   II. Liberalism, Conservatism and the State   9

  III. Justice and Equality   27

  IV. Two Contemporary Theories of Justice   39

    V. Justice and the Welfare State   59

  VI. Justice and the Bible   69

 VII. The Nature of Capitalism   81

VIII. Socialism   91

  IX. The Mixed Economy   103

    X. Is Capitalism Immoral?   111

  XI. Is Capitalism Irrational?   139

 XII. Liberation Theology   155

      Acknowledgments   169

      Bibliography   171

To
Kathy and Heidi
and
to the memory of their parents
Joyce and Keven Rose

Chapter One

The Two Faces
of Christian Social Concern

Thirty years ago or so, one often heard the claim that evangelical Christians had abandoned the arena of social action to theological liberals. One bit of evidence offered in support of this doubtful claim was the social gospel. Whether the assertion was ever really true, it is certainly not true today. Evangelicals have become increasingly involved in social action. They have come to recognize that as Christians they have an obligation to be concerned about more than the condition of their neighbor's soul. They understand their duty to be concerned about the plight of the poor, about social injustice, about urban blight, and about other issues of social significance.

As important as the social concern of the contemporary evangelical may be, it is only one side of the story. One of the two sides of Christian social concern *is* the Christian's clear obligation to care and to be concerned about the poor and oppressed and to do what he can on their behalf. But the other dimension of Christian social concern adds the stipulation that if a Christian wishes to make pronouncements on complex social, economic and political issues, he also has a duty to become informed about those issues. And that requires a careful study of economics and other social sciences. Many writings and speeches of Christian social activists evidence, for example, an inadequate grasp of economics. The late Benjamin Rogge, a professor of economics and Lutheran layman, lamented that

... the typical American who calls himself a Christian and who makes pronouncements ... on economic policies or institutions, does so out of an almost complete ignorance of the simplest and most widely accepted tools of economic analysis. If something arouses his Christian concern, he asks not whether it is water or gasoline he is tossing on the economic fire—he asks only whether it is a well-intended act. As I understand it, the Christian is required to use his God-given reason as well.[1]

Few Christians, whatever their political persuasion, have made the effort to study the foundational issues that underlie the problem of social justice. It is not enough to feel compassion for the poor and oppressed. Compassion and love must be coupled with a careful grounding in the relevant philosophical, economic, political and social issues.

If the evangelical social activist proceeds in ignorance of the accepted tools of economic analysis, he risks turning bad situations into something far worse. Witness for example, Ronald Sider's recent book, *Rich Christians in an Age of Hunger*, that gained wide acceptance among evangelical readers.[2] Many people were helped by that book to see the terrible plight of many of the world's poor. Sider had one side of the equation right: the Christian needs to care. Unfortunately, his book contained any number of proposals which, if put into effect, would subject the poor he was attempting to aid to even more serious economic devastation. For example, he suggested that Americans should unilaterally begin to pay more than a market price for certain commodities from poor countries. He seemed blissfully unaware of the long-range consequences such policies would have on the economy of poorer nations. But such economic short-sightedness did not escape the attention of George Mavrodes, a University of Michigan philosopher.

Sider usually seems unaware that his policies may have different results than he intends. Suppose that we [Americans] voluntarily

1. Benjamin Rogge, "Christian Economics: Myth or Reality?" *The Freeman*, December, 1965.
2. (Downers Grove, Illinois: Intervarsity Press, 1977).

increased the price that we pay for crude rubber (a recurrent suggestion of Sider's), then, Sider says, rubber workers would get higher wages. Fine. But wouldn't rubber producers scramble to increase production? And wouldn't land and labor be diverted from other enterprises, such as food production, to cash in on higher rubber prices? Since we don't need more rubber, the increased production would represent a waste of resources. Sider seems not to notice such consequences.[3]

Robert Frykenberg, a professor of history at the University of Wisconsin, is another evangelical critic of Sider. Writing in *Christianity Today*, Frykenberg points out that it is easy for theologians like Sider to announce that the world's poor need food and help. Sider stops short of the much more difficult task of describing some effective and realistic way of meeting those needs.

But without showing us exactly how the world's hungry are to be fed, nothing results except the mouthing of pious platitudes and highly emotional exhortations to act. Such well-meaning efforts to help are at best inefficient and wasteful, and, at worst, utterly self-defeating and demoralizing. Often, like the children's crusades, they end up doing more harm than good.[4]

Sider's book typifies the approach that many contemporary Christians take toward social problems. There is no question about the fact that they care. But their compassion is often wedded to a political and economic ideology that is long on heart and short on wisdom. The emotional side of Christian social concern—loving and caring—is only half the story. The best of intentions cannot actually aid the poor unless channeled into actions that are informed by sound economic theory and practice. When "aid" is grounded on bad economics, it will usually make any bad situation worse.

All of this obviously leads to the question, what exactly constitutes sound economic and social theory? It should come as

3. George Mavrodes, "On Helping the Hungry," *Christianity Today*, Dec. 30, 1977, p. 46. Mavrodes' entire article deserves a careful reading.
4. Robert Frykenberg, "World Hunger: Food is not the Answer," *Chrisitanity Today*, December 11, 1981, p. 36.

no revelation that this question is the basis of a dispute that divides Christians into several camps. It should also come as no surprise that these divisions parallel ideologies that separate non-Christian thinkers. There was a day—not too long ago actually—when the options thought live by evangelicals were few and fairly simple to identify. Some Christians were political conservatives while others were liberals. Hardly anyone knew for sure what these labels meant but conservatives and liberals had little difficulty applying the labels to the right people.

Suddenly the world has become a far more complex place. One can now hear evangelical Christians identifying themselves as socialists and, in the case of a few radicals, as Marxists. As Klaus Bockmuehl explains,

> Marxism in the West today has become a potent temptation for gifted, forward-looking young Christians, evangelicals among them. They are fascinated not so much by its radical secular humanism as by its socialism. Because evangelicals have little knowledge of Marxism, they identify Marxism with social reform and regard it as an energetic attempt to realize liberty, equality and fraternity or simply claim that Marxists are 'for the poor.'[5]

The present state of the evangelical debate is characterized by a noticeable swing to the left on the part of many evangelical intellectuals. Almost without exception, the major evangelical books about social justice that have appeared since 1960 have been authored by writers who reject and condemn political conservatism as a cruel, heartless and uncaring movement totally out of step with an informed biblical view. Most recent evangelical publications on the subject insist that the Christian's undisputed obligation to demonstrate love for the needy obliges him to adopt liberal statist means to aid the poor. This assertion is supplemented by allegations that because political conservativism lacks compassion for the poor and allegedly fails

5. Taken from *The Challenge of Marxism* by Klaus Bockmuehl. © 1980 by Intervarsity Christian Fellowship of the U.S.A. and used by permission of Intervarsity Press, Downers Grove, Illinois, 60615, U.S.A.

to support programs to alleviate poverty, hunger and need, it
is an unacceptable option for the evangelical.[6]

Basic to the theory of the evangelical Christian who finds
liberalism or socialism or even Marxism attractive is an appeal
to social justice. Lewis Smedes justifies his political liberalism
"not on the basis of compassion, but on the basis of justice."[7]
Vernon Grounds criticizes politically conservative Christians
for what he describes as their casual indifference to social
injustice.[8] Grounding one's own position on an appeal to social
justice carries a built-in advantage. As Antonio Martino points
out, the expression "social justice"

. . . owes its immense popularity precisely to its ambiguity and
meaninglessness. It can be used by different people, holding quite
different views, to designate a wide variety of different things.
Its obvious appeal stems from its persuasive strength, from its
positive connotation, which allows the user to praise his own ideas

6. Some recent books that illustrate how easily Christian sentiments can be
used to support collectivist policies are: J. Philip Wogaman, *The Great Economic
Debate: An Ethical Analysis* (Philadelphia: The Westminster Press, 1977); Larry
L. Rasmussen, *Economic Anxiety and Christian Faith* (Minneapolis: Augsburg,
1981); David M. Beckmann, *Where Faith and Economics Meet* (Minneapolis,
Augsburg, 1981); Stephen Charles Mott, *Biblical Ethics and Social Change* (New
York: Oxford University Press, 1982). Of these four authors, perhaps only Mott
(who teaches at Gordon-Conwell Divinity School) would insist on being called
an evangelical. While somewhat older evangelical criticisms of political conser-
vatism seldom demonstrated much competence in economics, their books did
repeat the charge that political conservatives lack compassion for the poor. Some
of these books include: Robert G. Clouse, *The Cross and the Flag* (Carol Stream:
Creation House, 1972); Richard V. Pierard, *The Unequal Yolk* (Philadelphia:
J.B. Lippincott, 1970); Vernon Grounds, *Evangelicalism and Social
Responsibility* (Scottsdale, PA: Herald Press, 1969); and Donald Dayton,
Discovering an Evangelical Heritage (New York: Harper and Row, 1976). It
is important to note that none of the books in this latter group evidence any
familiarity with the literature of responsible conservatism. They contain repeated
warnings about the dangers present in any alliance between Christianity and
political conservatism. But it is clear that what they call political conservatism
is some kind of radical extremism of the right that bears little resemblance to
the responsible conservatism that will be described in chapter two.

7. Lewis B. Smedes, "Where do we differ?" *The Reformed Journal*, May-June,
1966, p. 10.

8. Grounds, *Evangelicalism and Social Responsibility*, op. cit., p. 4.

and simultaneously express contempt for the ideas of those who don't agree with him.[9]

After all, if a political liberal praises social justice, it seems to follow that anyone who disagrees with him must favor injustice. Once this seed is planted, it is but a short step to the conclusion that anyone disagreeing with the liberal's noble goals must be dishonorable. Martino does not question the sincerity of those who appeal so fervently to social justice:

> It cannot be denied that advocates of 'social justice' are quite often motivated by lofty ideals. Such is the case, for example, of those who are genuinely concerned about poverty and the need to do something about it. Their sincere compassion for the poor is undoubtedly a noble sentiment, and it deserves respect and admiration. However, their belief that the way to help the poor is by remodelling the whole of society (according to their preferred general plan) is more likely to hurt everybody than to achieve their aim.[10]

Martino warns about the ease with which the phrase "social justice" can be used in support of political measures harmful to individual liberty:

> The expression 'social justice' is more popular among advocates of statism than it is among individualists, since it is often used to justify (and praise) faith in the omnipotence of government. In this respect, it is intended to provide the 'moral' justification for what Sir Karl Popper calls 'holistic social engineering.'[11]

Serious questions can be raised about the evangelical liberal's grasp of the complex social, political and economic foundations of justice. The liberal evangelical is often inattentive to important distinctions in the notion of justice; he fails to see how his claims draw him into an unavoidable and dangerous dependence upon a coercive state; he is blind to the fact that many of his

9. Antonio Martino, "The Myth of Social Justice," in *Three Myths* by Arnold Beichman, Antonio Martino and Kenneth Minogue (Washington: The Heritage Foundation, 1982) p. 23.

10. Ibid., p. 24.

11. Ibid., p. 23.

preferred programs to help the poor end up being self-defeating; and he is unaware of the confusion that pervades his interpretation of the biblical teaching about justice. It is important to challenge the liberal assumption that social, political and economic conservatism is necessarily tied to a lack of compassion for the poor. Many evangelicals who are politically conservative oppose liberalism because they believe it is clear that liberal programs end up doing far more harm than good to the poor.

This book's investigation of social justice and the Christian church will include explorations in the areas of political theory, social philosophy, economics and theology. Much of the political theory is found in chapter 2 which asks such questions as, What do the words "liberalism" and "conservatism" mean? What is the state and how does it differ from society? What is statism and how are liberal social policies supportive of statism?

Beginning with chapter 3, the subject turns to social philosophy as the book offers a philosophical analysis of the concept of justice. Various theories about the nature of justice, ancient and contemporary, will be considered. Some of the questions raised in chapters 3, 4 and 5 are: What is the relationship of justice to equality? Does justice require the redistribution of a society's wealth? Do the demands of justice support the contemporary welfare state?

Chapter 6 considers what the Bible teaches about justice. This book intentionally rejects any proof-text approach to its subject. Many other treatments of the topic purport to "discover" revealed truth about economic and social theory in the Bible and then deduce the appropriate applications of that truth to the contemporary scene. The great problem with the proof-text method is the extent to which the participants beg the question. In most cases, what happens is that the writer finds some passage in the Old Testament that relates to an extinct cultural situation. It is often the case that such passages are ambiguous enough to give any interpreter problems. But then before the reader knows it, that passage is used to prove the truth of socialism or capitalism. This book takes a totally different approach. It assumes the unity of all truth. Truth in any area of human knowledge will be consistent with truth in every other area. If the Word of God speaks clearly and decisively on a subject, the Christian is obliged to make his beliefs about economics and politics consistent with that teaching. If a particular economic or political theory is supported by good reasons and is regarded as true, then it ought to be consistent with revealed truth. If it isn't, some changes are in order. Chapter 6 will argue that a careful analysis of the Bible's teaching about justice fails to support the claims made by the Christian liberal.

Chapter 7 is the first of several devoted to economics. Something called capitalism is the favorite whipping boy of liberals, socialists and Marxists today. These chapters suggest that contemporary critics of capitalism don't always know what they're talking about. Surprisingly, many contemporary attacks on capitalism (like those found in the writings of many liberation theologians) never bother to define the term "capitalism." These chapters attempt to bring some order out of chaos by offering analyses of capitalism, socialism and the so-called mixed economy. Chapters 10 and 11 examine the most frequently cited objections to capitalism and find them wanting.

In the last chapter of the book, liberation theology is subjected to a careful examination. Many liberation theologians blame capitalism for the plight of the world's poor and view socialism as the savior of the poor. Various weaknesses of liberation theology are discussed and a proposal is offered for a new liberation theology that takes a more realistic approach toward economic realities and toward human nature.

Chapter Two

Liberalism, Conservatism and the State

Disagreements over social, political and economic theory divide Christians into several competing ideologies. To date, the most prominent of these ideologies among American Christians are *liberalism* and *conservatism*. Both words are difficult to define. One reason for this difficulty is the fact that the same words have been used to refer to significantly different belief systems in different centuries and different nations. Most students of social philosophy recognize that the classical liberalism of the nineteenth century and contemporary liberalism are two quite different movements. But not everyone can pinpoint the precise differences. Many people also sense that profound differences exist between contemporary American conservatism and what used to be called conservatism in the nineteenth century.

While contemporary American conservatism is an admittedly diverse movement, with several major branches, it nonetheless has a mainstream that can be identified. One way to get at the essence of this mainstream is to examine the relationship between nineteenth century conservatism and the classical liberalism of that century. In a sense, both of these older movements constitute smaller branches of contemporary conservative thought. That is, there are some American conservatives (Senator Barry Goldwater is often regarded as one example) who are really classical liberals. Other American conservatives like Russell Kirk are more at home with the traditional nineteenth century conservativism of Edmund Burke. But between the basically libertarian convictions of people like Goldwater on the one hand and the traditionalism of thinkers like Kirk on the other, there is a conservative mainstream that attempts to fuse the libertarian's concern for freedom with the traditionalist's interest in tradition and social order.

To a great extent, the nineteenth century struggle between conservative social thought and classical liberalism was a conflict between those traditionalists who stressed objective values and order, and the liberals who emphasized freedom and the importance of the individual. Surprisingly, a great many contemporary social theorists still cling to the dichotomy of freedom and virtue. Many who believe that the preservation of social order requires the observance of unchanging moral laws tend to view any emphasis on liberty as a threat. Many friends of freedom see any defense of moral order as an equally grave threat to their cause.

Nineteenth century conservatism deserves both praise and blame: praise for its clear affirmation that no society can survive if it repudiates the objective moral laws that provide the structure of social order, and blame for its frequent indifference to the cause of liberty. The situation was reversed in nineteenth century liberalism. While liberalism's commitment to freedom was admirable, its defense of liberty was inadequate. Most nineteenth century liberals tried to defend freedom on utilitarian grounds, which meant that the case for liberty depended entirely on freedom producing consequences of a certain kind, e.g., happiness for the greatest number of people. The utilitarian defense of liberty was weak since it would only work for those who shared the liberal's preferences for the ends of individual human beings over the ends of society. Grounding the case for liberty on nothing more substantial than human preference left open the possibility that utilitarians could disavow freedom should they become persuaded that their preferred ends could be attained more successfully through coercive measures. In fact, this was precisely the direction taken by the thought of John Stuart Mill. As Frank Meyer urged, there must be a stronger case for freedom.

> Freedom as an essential right of men is founded not upon preferences, but upon the nature of men and the very constitution of being. [Freedom] is inalienable and infeasible as a right, not for any reasons of utility but because it is the true condition of man's created being. In the argument with collectivism, utilitarian reason can always be answered with alternative utilitarian reasons. The final struggle with collectivism . . . can only be waged in terms of an understanding with the nature of man.[1]

Meyer came to see that freedom should not be viewed simply as a means to preferred ends. He believed that freedom must be grounded on a Christian view of being and man. Man's essential freedom and his right to exercise that freedom are his by virtue of his creation in God's image. To be truly human, to be most expressive of all the potential that being a carrier of the divine image implies, requires that human beings be free; they must be able to choose. When the state deprives man of his liberty, man loses an essential part of his humanness.

As noted, the first error of nineteenth century liberalism was its failure to ground human freedom in the nature of man's created being. The classical liberal's second mistake was the fear of acknowledging an objective and transcendent ground of value. Because utilitarianism was incompatible with unchanging moral ends, classical liberalism lacked an "ultimate sanction for the inviolability of the person" and was left without any foundation for "its defense of the person as primary in political and social matters."[2] As M. Stanton Evans observes, "If there is no value system with which we may rebuke the pretensions of despots, what is to prevent the rule of force in the world?

---

1. Frank Meyer, *The Conservative Mainstream* (New York: Arlington House, 1968) pp. 76, 77.
2. Frank Meyer, *Defense of Freedom*, (Chicago: Henry Regnery Co., 1962) p. 2.

If there are no objective standards of right and wrong, why object to tyranny?"[3] According to Meyer,

> The Christian understanding of the nature and destiny of man, which is the foundation of Western civilization, is always and everywhere what conservatives strive to conserve. That understanding accepts the existence of absolute truth and good and at the same time recognizes that men are created with the free will to accept or reject that truth and good. Conservatism, therefore, demands both the struggle to vindicate truth and good and the establishment of conditions in which the free will of individual persons can be effectively exercised.[4]

Meyer then agrees with Christian theism that freedom can only be defended in a context where men acknowledge the existence of objective and unchanging moral laws.

Meyer's use of the conservative label to identify his position may puzzle readers accustomed to equating conservatism with the authoritarian traditionalism of the nineteenth century conservatives or with the twentieth century disciples of Edmund Burke.[5] In the view of Meyer and many others, contemporary American conservatism should not be confused with nineteenth century traditionalism or, for that matter, with classical liberalism. Meyer believed that there is a center, a consensus, a mainstream of conservatism in America that is in fact a fusion of two streams of thought: the classical liberal's respect for the liberty of the individual person and the traditional conservative's respect for objective and unchanging moral values. As Meyer wrote,

> I believe that those two streams of thought, although they are sometimes presented as mutually incompatible, can in reality be united within a single broad conservative political theory, since

3. M. Stanton Evans, "A Conservative Case for Freedom," in *What is Conservatism?* ed. Frank Meyer (New York: Holt, Rinehart and Winston, 1965) p. 72.

4. Meyer, *Conservative Mainstream*, op. cit., p. 54.

5. Without question, the best known contemporary traditionalist is Russell Kirk. See his *The Conservative Mind* (South Bend: Regnery/Gateway, 1972).

they have their roots in a common tradition and are arrayed against a common enemy.[6]

Moreover, conservatives like Meyer believe their fusion of libertarianism and traditionalist concerns faithfully reflects the view of the founding fathers. Conservatives believe that the Constitution's program of protecting individual freedom in an ordered society governed by a limited state "was the closest that human beings have come to establishing a policy which gives the possibility of maintaining at one and the same time individual liberty, underlying norms of law, and necessary public order."[7] In a different book, Meyer drew the following conclusions:

> The American conservative has indeed a special heritage, the discussions and the achievements of the Founders of the American constitution (Madison preeminently), men who established the highest political form the West has yet created to express the tension of transcendent truth and human freedom. The political structure they left us has its contradictions, no doubt; but . . . they reflect the imperfect state of man and the tension within which he must live if he is to be true to his nature, striving towards transcendent ends in freedom.[8]

One can hardly be a conservative without something to conserve or defend. For the contemporary American conservative, that which he seeks to conserve is nothing less than the system of government that is the legacy of the American founding fathers. Inherent in that system and articulated in such works as *The Federalist Papers* are convictions about man and society that the conservative believes constitute the foundations of his

6. Frank Meyer, "Freedom, Tradition, Conservatism," in *What is Conservatism?* op. cit., p. 8.

7. Ibid., pp. 7-8. Compare also the following: "For ours is the most effective effort ever made to articulate in *political* terms the Western understanding of the interrelation of the freedom of the person and the authority of an objective moral order." Meyer, *Defense*, op. cit., p. 8.

8. Meyer, *Mainstream*, op. cit., p. 56. An excellent account of the diversity of conservative thought can be found in M. Stanton Evans' article, "Varieties of Conservative Experiences," *Modern Age*, Spring, 1971, pp. 130-137.

own political theory. For example, conservatives believe that one of their fundamental differences with liberalism is their opposition to what they see as a pervasive streak of utopianism in liberal social thought. Conservatives think that liberals consistently overestimated mankind's propensities for good and thus became infatuated with the basic error of utopianism, namely, the perfectibility of man and the possibility of a perfect society. As the conservative sees it, the twentieth century liberal is bewitched by the delusion that man is not really inherently evil. Liberals think that when a man errs, it is only because he has been corrupted by society. According to this view, the major hindrances to the attainment of a good society are human ignorance and inadequate social institutions. Evil is a result either of improper conditions in man's environment or of human ignorance (which is again the responsibility of society since it is supposed to alleviate this ignorance through education).

Conservatives will have none of this utopianism. While conservatives are no less interested in improving man's condition and his social institutions, they reject absolutely

> ... the idea that society or men generally are perfectible. In particular, [they are] perennially suspicious of the utopian approach that attempts to *design* society and the lives of human beings, whether in the light of abstract rationalist ideas or operational engineering concepts. [They] therefore reject the entire Liberal mystique of "planning," which, no matter how humanitarian the motives of the planners, perforce treats human beings as faceless units to be arranged and disposed according to a design conceived by the planner.[9]

It was because the framers of the Constitution believed that human nature could not be trusted that they created a complicated and cumbersome system of government in which various checks and balances serve to make the attainment of absolute power by any one man or group of men extremely

9. Frank Meyer, "Conservatism," in *Left, Right and Center*, ed. Robert A. Goldwin (Chicago: Rand McNally, 1967) pp. 6, 7.

difficult. "To expect self-denial from men," John Adams wrote, "when they have a majority in their favor and consequently power to gratify themselves is to disbelieve all history and universal experience; it is to disbelieve Revelation and the Word of God, which informs us the heart is deceitful in all things and desperately wicked." How then, given this more biblical and realistic view of human nature, can a free and orderly republic be maintained? Adams' answer was a series of checks and balances: "The essence of a free government consists in an effectual control of rivalries." Unchecked government is to be rejected regardless of whether it is the government of a king, an aristocracy, or an unrestrained majority. Even though government is necessary to control human passions and selfishness, government can itself become a menace should it grow too strong. As James Madison observed in *The Federalist* (#51):

> It may be a reflection on human nature, that such devices [as checks and balances] should be necessary to control the abuses of government. But what is government itself, but the greatest of all reflections on human nature? If men were angels, no government would be necessary. If angels were to govern men, neither external nor internal controls on government would be necessary.

But, of course, men are not angels, and since a government must be established, it must be a government which cannot abuse its authority. In Madison's words, "You must first enable the government to control the governed; and in next place oblige it to control itself."

Nineteenth century liberals like John Stuart Mill believed government should be limited because men are essentially good. American conservatives believe that government should be limited because men are evil. The conservative individualist is concerned to find a political system in which bad men can do the least amount of harm.

Political conservatives are sometimes known as individualists. This ambiguous label is best understood as an opposition to all forms of political collectivism. The fundamental error of collectivism is to assume that society is some kind of living organism and then treat this organism as the end or standard which decides all moral and political policy. In his concern for social wholes, the collectivist too readily allows the importance of the individual to be subordinated to the well-being of some larger group.[10]

Political conservatives and liberals in America also hold contrasting attitudes toward the state and statism. Because their different stances on this issue constitute perhaps the most important distinction between contemporary American conservatism and liberalism, the rest of this chapter will be devoted to an analysis of the issue. Two preliminary questions must be answered: What do we mean by the word "state"? and What is statism?

The state is simply another word for the group of individuals which actually runs a nation, makes its laws, issues its commands, punishes those regarded in violation of the rules, and acquires the money required to run the machinery of the state. Great harm can result from confusing the state with the totality of the people. The state is not identical with all the people. It is a separate group of people who possess a monopoly of legal coercive power. A state is not just an organized group of people located within some specified territorial boundary. Always, within each of these geographical groupings, the actual orders are issued by a much smaller group that makes the laws and forces the others to obey. The group that rules may be one or many. Its power will be sustained and enhanced by the support of a group of loyal followers; but the state itself is identical with the person or group that holds the power.

The state differs from society in at least one important respect. Society is marked by the *voluntary* character of its

10. The conservative opposition to collectivism is often misrepresented as an endorsement of social atomism. Political and social institutions simply could not exist nor could political theory have any meaning if men and women were to live their lives in isolation from each other in the manner idealized by social atomists. For the conservative, man still is a social animal who necessarily exists in many vital and varied relationships with other human beings.

associations whereas the state is always characterized by its use of force, by its unwillingness to depend upon the voluntary support of the people. Compulsion, while found in many societies, is not an *essential* feature of the kind of companionship found in a society. The associations that characterize the state, however, are not voluntary. The basic difference between a society and the state is the indispensable place of force and power in the latter. The state always supports its claim to the obedience of its followers through the use of force. Wherever the state exists, one will necessarily find coercion.

Given man's propensity to expand his power and abuse his authority, history contains repeated examples of how states have confiscated power away from society. Our name for this inordinate expansion of the state's power is statism. "Statism" and "anti-statism" are not easy terms to define. Neither is a simple or fixed position. One approach to clarifying the meaning of the two words is to imagine a continuum with statism on one end and anti-statism on the other.

ANTI-STATISM			STATISM
0			100
Anarchism (total repudiation of the state)	the minimal state	the maximal state	Totalitarianism

The more extreme statism becomes, the more it approximates the evils of totalitarianism. Radical statists tend to view the state as an end in itself rather than as a means to achieving the ends of individual human beings. Frequently, extreme statists hypostatize what is nothing more than a set of relationships among many individual human beings into an existing being or organism that has its own life, moral duties, and rights. Some radical statists like Hegel have gone so far as to deify the state. In its fascist forms, statism asserts that the individual is nothing, while the state is everything. While Karl Marx may have longed for an eventual non-statist socialism, the Marxist nations of today cling to a totalitarian state socialism that is every bit as destructive of individual liberty as the statism of the fascist.

Referring back to the diagram given earlier and the continuum it pictures between statism and anti-statism, it seems fair to regard American liberalism as a type of humanitarian statism. "Humanitarian" refers to liberalism's intended ends while "statism" identifies the dominant features of the means it uses to reach those ends. In other words, contemporary American liberals believe their goal is improving the lot of the majority of people in their society; but they also believe the best means to achieve that end is granting the state the power necessary to bring about their objective.

Statism attracts converts for a variety of reasons. Some men simply lust for power and statism provides the quickest and most convenient route to the attainment of power. But many have turned to statism on allegedly humanitarian grounds. Contemporary political liberalism is simply the most influential manifestation of the humanitarian form of statism in this century. The liberal approach to social justice is a logical extension of the primacy it gives the state. The contemporary liberal statist contends that the freedom of many Americans is threatened because of the state's inability or refusal to become more active. Moreover, the liberal claims, many people need deliverance from the debilitating effects of poverty, ignorance, and the corrupting influence of big business. Only a powerful (and hopefully benevolent) state can provide this needed protection and can furnish a framework within which "genuine freedom" can thrive.

As some liberal writers see it, true freedom involves more than being free from constraints and coercion. True freedom also requires the ability or the power to do or to be certain things. And so, the liberal believes, the state must take action in order to enhance positive freedom. Millions of Americans are supposed to be living in literal bondage, not because America is a police state or because assorted coercive powers restrain them in some way, but simply because there are many things they are powerless to do or have. For anyone who believes this, it is a short step to the conclusion that the state must step in and help these people, because only then can they become truly free.

A similar bias in favor of the state infuses much liberal thinking about justice. Once "justice" is understood in its distributive sense, as related to the way goods and burdens are distributed within a society, the entrance of the state into such considerations is inevitable. Clearly, statism is a powerful force in much current U.S. political thought. And one of its more important justifications is the claim that the demands of justice naturally support and, indeed, require statist action. In his desire to achieve his social goals by the quickest possible means, the contemporary liberal concentrates as much power as possible in the one institution able to override all obstacles, the state. Given the recent dominance of liberalism in the political life of America, and given its reliance upon statist solutions to social and political problems, it is only natural that social justice has come to be viewed as inseparable from statist action. However the liberal construes the problems of his nation, however compassionate and altruistic his professed goals, he believes those objectives can only be attained through the instrument of statist power.

The contemporary conservative believes he has a more realistic view of human nature and thus recognizes more clearly than the liberal the dangers involved in vesting so much power in the hands of the state. The conservative believes in the importance of justice although he most certainly understands it differently, as we shall see. He also shares a differing concept of liberty, believing that human beings are most free when they are not subject to the will and coercion of others. For the conservative, the quest for a good society depends on a proper balance among a number of competing values, among which are freedom, justice and order. The attitude toward the state most compatible with conservative values is a form of minimal statism. The conservative is not an anarchist; he recognizes the need for a limited state.

It is important to distinguish two quite different types of anti-statism. (1) Radical anti-statism is opposed to any and every state; it attacks the state per se. Many anti-statists in this first sense openly embrace or at least look longingly on anarchism. Even when a radical anti-statist concludes that he cannot accept anarchism, he accepts the legitimacy of a minimal or limited state begrudgingly. (2) Moderate anti-statism is not opposed to the state per se; its attacks are directed against a particular kind of state, that is, the state that refuses to observe the rule of law,[11] that attempts to usurp more and more power away from societies, that continues to expand its coercive powers at the expenses of societal relationships. Moderate anti-statists oppose those states that seek to attack or undermine the voluntary communal dimensions of an individual's life, that usurp

11. What is often called "the Rule of Law" is one of the most important limitations on governmental power. The rule of law is found whenever the agents and arbiters in a situation are bound in advance by fixed and stated rules or laws. Within the limits of the rules, men are free to act to the best of their ability. Of course, some play the game better than others and are rewarded more lucratively. Our freedoms come into conflict with the liberties of others and with the limitations imposed by our circumstances and abilities. In order to preserve order amidst these conflicting claims, the state is given the monopoly of coercive power within its sphere of control. But it is vital in any free society that the power of the state be limited to laws which the citizen knows in advance. When the actions of the government are not announced in advance in the form of laws, it is impossible for the citizen to predict what the government will do or demand in any given situation. Thus the citizen's liberty is restricted because he cannot plan his own future actions, given his uncertainty about what the state will approve or condemn the next hour, day, or week. Where governments observe the rule of law, individuals can predict how the state will use its coercive powers in given circumstances and can thus govern their lives in a manner that will enable them to avoid penalties for improper conduct. Once the individual knows the rules of the game, he is free to pursue his personal ends so long as they do not conflict with the pre-announced rules. The rule of law prevents the state from taking ad hoc, arbitrary, and discriminatory action. Obviously, the rule of law is only a necessary but not a sufficient condition for liberty. Unjust laws could also deprive citizens of important liberties.

the functions of voluntary human associations. Moderate anti-statists are supportive of states that recognize the point at which their power is limited by the social sphere which, of course, includes both the family and the church. The minimal state recommended by contemporary conservatives is *not* the night watchman state of nineteenth century classical liberalism. The classical liberal state had only three basic functions: (1) the protection of its citizens from the threat of foreign invasion; (2) the protection of the rights of its citizens from violence or fraud or other wrongful interference; (3) the provision of a recognized authority with sufficient force to judge in conflicts between the rights of individuals. These are all necessary functions of any state. But the minimal state of the contemporary conservative has functions that go beyond national defense and the provision of law and order. Since laws must be changed to fit changing conditions, there must be a way in which the rules by which society operates can be changed. There must be some way of settling disagreements over the meaning of the rules. It is important to notice the additional roles that strong anti-statists like Friedrich Hayek and Milton Friedman are willing to assign to the minimal state. For example, Friedman writes:

A government which maintained law and order, defined property rights, served as a means whereby we could modify property rights and other rules of the economic game, adjudicated disputes about the interpretations of the rules, enforced contracts, promoted competition, provided a monetary framework, engaged in activities to counter technical monopolies and to overcome neighborhood effects widely regarded as sufficiently important to justify government intervention, and which supplemented private charity and the private family in protecting the irresponsible, whether madman or child—such a government would clearly have important functions to perform.[12]

12. Milton Friedman, *Capitalism and Freedom* (Chicago: University of Chicago Press, 1962) p. 34. For samples of Hayek's position, see Vol. III of his *Law, Legislation and Liberty* (Chicago: University of Chicago Press, 1979) pp. 41ff.

Such a minimal state would recognize and respect the fact that its power must not negate the important role that voluntary communities play with regard to the individual.

THE STATE AND THE NEW TESTAMENT

For the sake of completeness, a possible objection must be considered. Many sincere Christians might object to the critical stance this chapter has taken to the state on the grounds that it is incompatible with the basic New Testament passage on the subject, Romans 13:1-7.

> Let every person be subject to the governing authorities. For there is no authority except from God, and those that exist have been instituted by God. Therefore he who resists the authorities resists what God has appointed, and those who resist will incur judgment. For rulers are not a terror to good conduct, but to bad. Would you have no fear of him who is in authority? Then do what is good, and you will receive his approval, for he is God's servant for your good. For if you do wrong, be afraid, for he does not bear the sword in vain; he is the servant of God to execute his wrath on the wrongdoer. Therefore one must be subject, not only to avoid God's wrath but also for the sake of conscience. For the same reason you also pay taxes, for the authorities are ministers of God, attending to this very thing. Pay all of them their dues, revenue to whom revenue is due, respect to whom respect is due, honor to whom honor is due.[13]

Problems result if this passage is taken as an endorsement of statism or as the exclusive and final New Testament teaching about the state. The passage clearly teaches that the state plays an important function in providing for social order. But the previous argument has already acknowledged that point several times. A Christian anarchist interested in reconciling his view with the New Testament would have some major difficulties with the text. But anarchism has already been disqualified as

---

13. Romans 13:1-7, *The Revised Standard Version*, copyrighted by the Division of Christian Education of the National Council of the Churches of Christ in the U.S.A.

chapter offered an analysis of contemporary American conservatism and liberalism. The mainstream of contemporary American conservatism is understood best as a fusion of classical liberalism's concern with individual liberty and nineteenth century conservatism's concern with moral absolutes and social order. Conservatives are suspicious of attempts to solve social problems by granting additional powers to government. Anxious to conserve the political convictions that gave birth to the U.S. Constitution, convictions expressed in the views of such founding fathers as James Madison and John Adams, the conservative is a moderate anti-statist in the sense that he recognizes the continuing importance of checks and limits on governmental power. As conservatives view the liberal enterprise, the liberal is willing to forego some of these restraints on the size and power of government in order to realize more quickly and, the liberal thinks, more effectively, his humanitarian goals. The conservative does not necessarily object to the liberal's ends; but as we shall see, he does believe the liberal's choice of ends is often self-defeating and dangerous.

Chapter Three

Justice and Equality

The claim that social justice requires the necessary support and active intervention of a large, powerful and paternalistic state is an essential part of the liberal political creed in America. According to that creed, the forcible imposition of new social policy is justified on the ground that it is mandated by the demands of social justice. Only an increase in the size and power of the state, only a greater concentration of power in the central government, the liberal believes, can provide a framework within which justice can thrive.

Some conservatives see a similarity between the contemporary liberal's appeal to justice and the situation that prevailed in the city-state of Athens more than 2400 years ago. In ancient Athens, Socrates attempted to warn his contemporaries of the dangers involved in grounding drastically new social policies on unanalyzed concepts. Socrates saw the leaders of his community attempt to slip questionable and dangerous policies past the inattentive masses through the use of ambiguous terms like "justice." America's political liberals emulate the enemies of Socrates to the extent that they seek to rally converts to their cause in the name of an undefined notion of justice. Every time an increase in our nation's governmental bureaucracy is recommended, every time some new political action in support of some special interest is advocated, the appeal to social justice is present somewhere in the neighborhood. But no one ever seems to ask what, if anything, the expression "social justice" means. Presumably intelligent people are frequently seen debating whether social justice requires this or that particular action; but seldom do the participants in these disputes raise the more fundamental question of what the phrase means. Attempts to analyze the meaning of justice are noticeably absent in most Christian discussions of social justice. Many contemporary Christian social activists simply assume that when they claim that justice demands this action or that policy, everyone knows precisely what the term means. A careful analysis of "justice" will help to reveal the specious character of most liberal appeals to the term. The word has several functions ranging from its use as a synonym for righteousness to more particular usages in which people receive their due in commercial, remedial and distributive situations.[1] Several chapters will be spent exploring the various nuances of the term "justice." The remainder of this chapter will examine the frequently made claim that just treatment is equal treatment, that justice and equality are equivalent notions, a view that plays a central role in much liberal thinking about justice.

SOME IMPORTANT LESSONS FROM THE CLASSICAL ANALYSIS OF JUSTICE

A logical starting point for any discussion of justice is the treatment of the subject in the writing of classical philosophers. Several points made in Aristotle's examination of the topic are relevant to the contemporary debate.

I. *Justice and a person's due*

The ancients believed that justice always involves giving a

---

1. Some participants in the debate about justice warn about a clever semantic manuever by the statist that makes his case appear much more plausible than it really is. The cunning strategy attempts to obscure the differences between "justice" and "social justice." It allows the statist to slide conveniently between the positive emotive appeal of the first term and the ambiguous, controversial meaning of the second.

person his due, that to which he has a right. The reason why a person may be due something varies with his or her situation. A hypothetical person named Jones would be due something in each of the following cases:

(1) If Jones does better work than any other student in the class, she is due the best grade.

(2) If Jones is the prettiest contestant in a beauty contest, she is due first prize.

(3) If Jones is the first to finish a race, she is due the prize.

(4) If Jones is promised something by Smith, Jones is due the fulfillment of that promise.

(5) If Jones' property is stolen or damaged by Smith, Jones is due whatever reparation is required to restore what she lost.

The what and why of any person's due cannot be reduced to a single formula of the form, to each according to his _____. Many attempts have been made to complete this phrase with terms like ability, need and achievement. But each of these criteria would fit some situations and not others. However much the determination of a person's due varies with the situation, it seems clear that the essence of justice involves each person having or receiving that which he is due. However complex the total analysis of justice may become, any adequate inquiry must retain this ancient insight. At the very least, justice occurs in situations where people receive what they are due. In any case where someone is denied what he or she is due, an injustice has occurred.[2]

II. *The universal and particular senses of justice*

One of the great virtues of Aristotle's discussion of "justice" was his attempt to distinguish the more important meanings of the word. As Aristotle saw it, a person can be said to be just in two quite different senses.[3] The first of these, *universal*

2. But, of course, one thing that complicates discussions about justice is disagreement over whether a particular person is due something.
3. Aristotle's examination of justice is found in Book Five of his *Nichomachean Ethics*.

justice, is coextensive with the whole of righteousness, with the whole of virtue. A person is just in the universal sense if he possesses all the proper virtues, if he is moral, if he keeps the laws, which Aristotle thought should accord with virtuous behavior. A soldier who runs away from the enemy during a battle is unjust in this universal sense. So too is a husband who is unfaithful to his wife or who fails to provide for his family. The just man in Aristotle's universal sense is the one who acts virtuously toward others.

The Bible also utilizes this universal sense of justice. It is present in Genesis 6:9 where Noah is described as a just man who is perfect in all his ways. In Ezekial 18:5, the just man is defined as one who does that which is lawful and right. In fact, the vast majority of biblical allusions to justice appear to be examples of justice in this universal sense.[4] Attention to this fact is important because many who are anxious to find biblical support for socialist policies quote many of these passages about justice. Read carefully, however, the texts are irrelevant to their purposes.

A person is just in the classical universal sense if he is virtuous and keeps the laws of his country (Aristotle), if he keeps the commandments of God (the Old Testament), if he is kind and charitable, if he provides for his family, if he helps the poor; in other words, if he manifests the virtues normally associated with being a moral or righteous person.

III. *The major kinds of particular justice*

Aristotle recognized that "justice" may also be used in the sense of *particular justice*. In this particular sense of the word, a man is just if he treats other people fairly, if he does not grasp

---

4. See Jer. 9:24; II Sam. 23:3; Prov. 20:7; Isa. 26:7; Ps. 82:3; Micah 6:8; Job 29:14-17; II Cor. 9:8-10; and so on. Eric Beversluis has accused this list of Scriptural passages of being "highly selective." He seems unaware of the fact that these are the very passages that liberal evangelicals and liberation theologians have cited. See Eric Beversluis, "Christianity, Economic Justice, and the State," *Christian Scholars' Review*, Fall, 1982. See my reply in the same issue.

after more than he is due. Aristotle distinguished three kinds of particular justice:

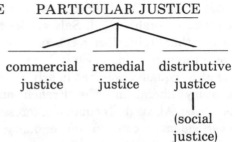

UNIVERSAL JUSTICE   PARTICULAR JUSTICE

commercial   remedial   distributive
justice   justice   justice
                            (social
                            justice)

(1) Interpersonal relations involving economic exchanges raise questions of *commercial justice*. When people exchange goods and services, questions arise as to whether the exchange is fair or the compensation just. Passages of Scripture like Leviticus 19:36 and Proverbs 16:11 that oblige merchants to have just scales and weights seem directed to this type of justice.

(2) Instances where some wrong must be made right under either criminal or civil law are occasions for *remedial justice*. Cases where an innocent individual is found guilty or where the punishment for an offense is too severe or too lenient are instances of injustice in this sense. Exodus 23:3-6 is one of a number of biblical passages that speaks to issues of remedial justice.

(3) Finally, questions about *distributive justice* arise in situations where some good or burden is apportioned among human beings. Such situations are encountered frequently as, for example, when a parent divides the evening dessert among the members of a large family, or a man divides his estate among his heirs. As the term is used in contemporary writings, *social justice* is viewed as that species of distributive justice concerned with the distribution of burdens and benefits within society as a whole, a distribution that is usually controllable by political authorities.

THE RELATION BETWEEN JUSTICE AND EQUALITY

Many people think that justice and equality are equivalent notions. Contemporary liberals view equality as an unqualified good. Richard Wollheim calls equality "the fundamental principle of Liberalism."[5] J. Salwyn Schapiro agrees and goes on to add that "Liberalism has proclaimed the principle of equality for all human beings everywhere."[6] This categorical endorsement of equality was not nearly so widespread in nineteenth century liberalism. The French author of *Democracy in America*, Alexis de Tocqueville, foresaw the possibility that the ever-widening concern for equality in America could blur important distinctions in human talent. He warned of the possibility that a majority of citizens might achieve economic and social equality at the cost of conformity in taste and thought. Such equality would also conflict with freedom. If the state is to guarantee that people are equal, it will have to interfere in their lives, often using coercion when they are unwilling to submit to the state's plan. One of the basic human liberties, de Tocqueville believed, was the freedom to be different from other people. How can this freedom be compatible with a state-imposed egalitarianism? De Tocqueville also pointed out one major reason for the popularity of egalitarian measures. While the value of egalitarian acts always appears rather quickly, it often takes a great deal of time for the resultant abuses of freedom to become apparent.

The liberal's ideological attachment to equality may account for the infrequency with which his convictions on the subject are supported with arguments. As Nozick observes:

> The legitimacy of altering social institutions to achieve greater equality of material condition is, though often assumed, rarely *argued* for. . . . It cannot merely be *assumed* that equality must be built into any theory of justice. There is a surprising dearth of arguments for equality capable of coming to grips with the

5. Richard Wollheim, "Equality," *Aristotelian Society Supplement*, 1956, p. 300.

6. J. Salwyn Schapiro, *Liberalism: Its Meaning and History* (Princeton, New Jersey: D. Van Nostrand Co., 1958) p. 10.

considerations that underlie a . . . nonpatterned conception of justice in holdings. (However, there is no lack of unsupported statements of a presumption in favor of equality.)[7]

As before, the writings of Aristotle are a good place to begin an exploration of the relationship between justice and equality. For Aristotle, the basic principle of all just action (in the particular sense of justice) is summarized in the statement that equals should be treated equally and unequals unequally. Injustice always exists when similar people are treated differently or when dissimilars are treated alike. Chaim Perelman has referred to Aristotle's formula as the Formal Principle of Justice.[8] While the Formal Principle is, many believe, a necessary condition for any just action, its admirers are quick to admit the deficiences of the principle. For one thing, it is not a sufficient principle of justice. That is, conformity to it will not guarantee justice. For example, a society might decide to treat all members of a particular class alike, but badly. Like treatment of likes can be unjust if the criteria by which people are grouped into classes are discriminatory and irrelevant to their claims to justice. The most serious weakness of the so-called Formal Principle of Justice is the absence of a criterion to identify which of the many ways people can be compared are relevant to questions of justice. If one is judging a beauty contest or assigning grades in a philosophy class or deciding the winner of an election, the factors that should count in each case are both different and fairly obvious. It is unlikely that a young lady's inability to write a good philosophy essay will disqualify her from a beauty contest whereas size fifteen feet might.

Something else must be added to the Formal Principle to complete the picture of justice and identify the revelant respects in which similarities require similar treatment. Aristotle

7. Robert Nozick, *Anarchy, State and Utopia*, (New York: Basic Books, 1974) pp. 232f. Some of the terms Nozick uses in this paragraph will be explained in the next chapter.
8. Chaim Perelman, *The Idea of Justice and the Problem of Argument* (New York: Humanities Press, 1963) chapter one.

believed that human equality and inequality should count only in instances where the similarity or difference is relevant to what is being distributed. While the parentage of a flute player is not relevant to the distribution of flutes, musical ability is. It is not enough to add up the ways in which human beings are equal or unequal. One must count only those respects that are relevant to what is being distributed. Aristotle's discussion suggests that "equality" may be as slippery a term as "freedom" and "justice." Aristotle's principle leaves open the possibility of discriminatory treatment. Similar people in similar situations should be treated alike. But the presence of relevant differences also mandates different treatment. Left unstated is a principle to identify which differences should count as grounds for unequal treatment.

In an effort to supplement the Formal Principle, some philosophers have sought a *material* principle of justice that would supply criteria for justifying dissimilar treatment. A number of these proposed material principles are clearly inadequate. For example, many possible bases of unequal treatment are unacceptable because they are factors for which no one can claim responsibility or credit. This consideration has been used to rule out all attempts to ground a distribution on criteria like sex, race, height, or eye color. Other possible criteria for unequal treatment like wealth, power, and social position have been disqualified because they depend upon earlier distributions which themselves may have been unjust. Critics of such a view hold that no theory of distribution can be acceptable which is based upon some feature which may have resulted from unjust human action. Clearly, they think, a person's sex or race or wealth or power or social position should not be used as the basis on which he or she receives a larger or smaller share of what is distributed.

The most promising candidates for a material principle of justice are well-known. They include such factors as ability, past achievement, effort, need, merit, and desert. Depending on the context, the application of any of these criteria *might* be correct.

If it is medical care that is being distributed, the health needs of the patient are relevant. If a parent is distributing praise to his children, the deeds or effort of the child are relevant. The distribution of wages is often pertinent to a laborer's work. Great difficulties result from the attempt to elevate any one of these principles to the exclusion of the others. No single all-embracing material principle of distribution can possibly be adequate. Sometimes need is relevant, but not always. Sometimes, but not always, merit should count.

Some evangelicals have recently advanced need as the ultimate material principle of justice. Robert K. Johnston claims that the biblical definition of justice is "to each according to his or her needs."[9] Johnston criticizes other norms of justice as secular in origin, as an intrusion of secular ideologies into what should be an exclusively biblical position. It is ironic that his own formulation of justice, which he insists is not derived from some secular ideology, is simply a paraphrase of that offered by Marx. The unsoundness of all attempts to push one exclusive principle invalidates need as the dominant factor affecting dissimilar distributions. Sometimes inequalities based on need are just; but many times they are not. A just distribution of grades for a college course should have nothing to do with whether a student "needs" a particular grade. In this case, the just grade should be asssigned on the basis of what the student has earned, not what he needs. The notion of "need" is extremely ambiguous. People "need" things for many different reasons. A student may feel he needs a particular grade in order to qualify for the football team, in order to graduate, in order to continue on the dean's list so as to qualify for a scholarship, or to increase the student's self-esteem. However much sympathy such needs may generate, they should not be relevant in cases like this. Many believe, perhaps rightly, that a good society will not allow certain fundamental and essential human needs to go unmet while a surplus exists. Unfortunately

9. Robert K. Johnston, *Evangelicals at an Impasse* (Atlanta: John Knox Press, 1979) p. 98.

need is too elastic a concept to serve as the precise standard required for distributive justice. Needs have a way of being generated and expanded as people become accustomed to former luxuries. If need is to function as one of the several material principles of justice, society must find some way to identify the essential needs in the given situation. It is also unclear whether the efforts of a society to meet such essential needs should be described as justice or charity.

George Mavrodes notes one important consideration that precludes "any simple passage from justice to equality, or vice versa."

> Any policy or pattern of action which we can plausibly defend or recommend on the grounds of equality can also be plausibly attacked and rejected on the grounds of inequality. . . . if equality is applied to unequals the results are unequal. But human beings and their works are the focus of profound inequalities. Any policy, therefore, which is from one point of view a policy of equal treatment must be from another point of view a sort of unequal treatment. So, if equal opportunities are provided to people with unequal abilities, then the results will predictably be unequal. If, on the other hand, one assigns opportunities in such a way as to generate equal results, then there must be inequalities in the allotment of the opportunities. This sort of factor seems almost painfully evident in the controversies surrounding the recent Bakke case, and the policy of preferential college admissions in general. Each side defends its own preferred policy in terms of equality, and attacks that of its adversary in terms of its inequality.[10]

Mavrodes' remarks suggest the importance of distinguishing between an egalitarianism of results and an egalitarianism of means. To the extent that any state attempts to produce equal results, it will have to treat people differently. But if the egalitarian abandons his quest for equal results and concentrates instead on equal treatment (means), he must then be content with the unequal results that will follow. As Mavrodes

10. George Mavrodes, "Morality, Equality and the Public Order," unpublished paper delivered at Hillsdale College, Hillsdale, Michigan, p. 5. The paper is copyrighted by the college's Center for Constructive Alternatives, 1979.

observes, "there is not, and cannot be, any public policy which generates equality along all of the important dimensions in which we have an interest."[11]

The contemporary obsession with equality gives rise to other difficulties. Most forms of egalitarianism tend to a type of social leveling. Because some people can never be elevated to the level of those with superior intelligence or ability or greater motivation, the concern for equality frequently results in the most gifted being forced to a lower level. This is harmful to society over the long run. While each person should be given an equal chance to enjoy the best possible life, it is sometimes necessary to give extra attention to the especially gifted. Since the gifted are often people who lead society, aiding them helps all within society. At the very least, society should place no obstacles in the path of the more gifted. In a free society where people are not restrained from helping themselves, the gifted will naturally be better achievers. Those who argue that it is unjust for society to do anything extra for gifted individuals who are able to achieve a better life until all have been brought up to their highest possible level (an impossible ideal, to be sure) ignore the role that the gifted can play in raising the level of the rest of society.

What should Christians learn from a study of classical discussions of justice? (1) Justice occurs in situations where people receive their due. (2) Distributive justice occurs in situations where equals are treated equally and unequals are treated unequally. (3) But this knowledge won't get us very far until we discover some principle that will tell us the relevant respects on which equal and unequal treatment should be based. (4) Several clearly inappropriate material principles of justice were identified. (5) The criteria that may be appropriate are many and varied. No one of them will work in every case. (6) While much about the notion of justice remains unclear, it is certain that justice and equality are not equivalent.

11. Ibid., p. 6.

Sometimes equal treatment is just; often it is not. Frequently, justice will require that people be treated differently.

Chapter Four

Two Contemporary Theories
Of Justice

In the past decade, two important new books on the nature of justice have appeared, both written by professors of philosophy at Havard University. John Rawls' book, *A Theory of Justice*,[1] was published in 1971 while Robert Nozick's *Anarchy, State and Utopia*[2] appeared in 1974. Contemporary liberals found many aspects of Rawls' position conducive to their viewpoint while libertarians and other less radical anti-statists welcomed many of Nozick's arguments. Given the prominent place that both books have had in recent discussions about justice, there is merit in seeing how the positions of Rawls and Nozick apply to the evangelical debate about justice.[3]

RAWLS ON JUSTICE

It is rather ironic that a work acclaimed by many as a modern philosophic classic should nonetheless lead its readers to extremely diverse interpretations. Daniel Bell praised the book as "the most comprehensive effort in modern philosophy to

1. John Rawls, *A Theory of Justice* (Cambridge: Harvard University Press, 1971).
2. Robert Nozick, *Anarchy, State and Utopia* (New York: Basic Books, 1974).
3. Because of the size of the two books (Rawls' book contains 607 pages), the complexity of their arguments, and our own spatial limitations, it should be obvious that only a brief summary of some of their more important points is possible.

justify a socialistic ethic."⁴ The anti-socialist, Friedrich Hayek, believed Rawls to be a supporter of his own type of individualism.⁵ The libertarian philosopher, John Hospers, is convinced that "Rawls' just society turns out to conform to the ideals of a moderately left-leaning member of the Democratic Party."⁶

Some rather obvious inconsistencies in Rawls' over-all position are evident. For example, Rawls himself regarded his book as a rejection of utilitarian views of justice; yet his own theory appears to be a forward-looking theory that ties justice to the consequences of certain actions.⁷ There is deserved punch in the observation of the British philosopher, R. M. Hare, that Rawls' book makes one feel as though his ideas, like sand along the seashore, keep slipping through one's fingers. Drawing attention to the book's many repetitions, Hare notes that it is "seldom clear whether the repetitions really are *repetitions*, or modifications of previously expressed views."⁸ It is likely that selected passages from Rawls' book could be used to defend any one of several different theories of justice. While Rawls most likely is a liberal with definite statist leanings, his book can be read as supportive of several different approaches to the subject.

One of the original features of Rawls' book is a device he introduces to support two principles of justice he advocates. The device, similar to the state of nature theory found in the writings of Hobbes, Locke, and Rousseau, requires that anyone desiring to discover the principles needed to make a society just, should imagine himself in an original situation where no state exists.

4. Daniel Bell, "On Meritocracy and Equality," *Public Interest*, 1972, p. 72.

5. Friedrich Hayek, *Law, Legislation and Liberty*, Vol. II (Chicago: University of Chicago Press, 1976) p. 100. Hayek's statement is one of the most puzzling he has ever written.

6. John Hospers, a review of *A Theory of Justice* in *The Freeman*, December, 1973, p. 753.

7. This point is explained further in the discussion of Nozick's position which follows.

8. R. M. Hare, "Rawls' Theory of Justice," *The Philosophical Quarterly*, 1973, p. 251.

If a group of people, living without a state, had the power to plan for the organization of a government, Rawls thinks it is instructive to note precisely what principles of justice they would select. In order to make the choices of the people in this Rawlsian state of nature more significant, Rawls insists that their knowledge must be limited in a number of important respects. If the people knew what situations they would occupy once the state was organized, it is likely they would vote for principles of justice that would benefit themselves. That is, if they were men, they might vote for principles that would discriminate in favor of men. If they were in line for a large inheritance, their principles of justice might rule out or minimize inheritance taxes. If they knew they were going to be poor or handicapped, they might favor principles of justice that would work to the advantage of people in these classes. Therefore, Rawls draws what he calls "the veil of ignorance." We must assume, he says, that the people in the state of nature know nothing about their wealth, talents, occupations, race, sex, or anything else that might prejudice their selection of the principles of justice. Once the slate is wiped clean, once people in theory know absolutely nothing about their personal destiny in the new society, the principles of justice are exactly the principles any rational people would select, if they were indeed behind a veil of ignorance. From his original situation, Rawls adopts two principles of justice:

(1) Each person is to have an equal right to the most extensive basic liberty compatible with a similar liberty for others.
(2) Social and economic inequalitites are to be arranged so that they are both (a) reasonably expected to be to everyone's advantage, and (b) attached to positions and offices open to all.[9]

Rawls sometimes describes his position as a theory of "Justice as Fairness." He means that his two principles have to be regarded as fair since they are precisely the principles any reasonable person behind the veil of ignorance would adopt. The

9. Rawls, op. cit., p. 60.

first principle is egalitarian. Every person has an equal right to as much freedom as is compatible for everyone else. The second principle states when deviations from the principle of equal liberty are justified: namely, only in cases when there is a reasonable expectation that those inequalities will work to the advantage of everyone, and when the unequal positions and offices are open to all.

Obviously, a 600 page book has a great deal more to say about justice, but what seems to be the heart of Rawls' system has been summarized. The difficulties that arise from just these few paragraphs are enough to cast doubt on the soundness of Rawls' approach. For one thing, Rawls never provides arguments to support his identification of the two principles of justice. His case rests on his confidence that reasonable readers will end up intuiting principles of justice identical with his own. This seems a rather shaky foundation for such a massive system.

Rawls repeatedly emphasizes the virtues of his veil of ignorance. His system is founded on the conviction that anyone in the original position who is subjected to the epistemological limitations of the veil of ignorance would select precisely his two principles. Brian Barry, one of Rawls' more astute critics, has observed that just because some principle of justice was adopted in a Rawlsian state of nature, it does not follow that the principle would be just. Barry asks us to imagine two men, one white and the other black, who find themselves in an original situation like Rawls describes. Behind the veil of ignorance, neither can know his own race. Suppose further, Barry continues, that in all other respects (ability, intelligence, training) the two men are equal. Imagine that they are given a choice between two situations. In the first, they both earn $100 a week. In the second, both would earn much more money. One of them would earn $1000 a week while the other earned $500 a week. Suppose they were told that the difference in salary would be based entirely on race; that is the white man would earn twice as much as the black man. But the black man in the second situation would still earn five times as much as either man in the first situation. Barry reminds us that neither individual knows whether he will be the white or the black man. But whichever he is, he will earn at the very least five times more money. Which of the two situations would reasonable people select? Clearly, the second. But, Barry objects, this would result in reasonable people in a Rawlsian state of nature making a choice that is clearly unjust. It is unjust because the distribution is based solely on racial grounds. Therefore, Barry concludes, the principles that reasonable people would adopt in a Rawlsian original situation would not necessarily be just.[10]

Exception can also be taken to Rawls' principle that inequalities are justified only if they increase or do not decrease the advantages of the least advantaged members of society. John Hospers provides a damaging example:

> Suppose that the distribution of goods in a society (which for the sake of simplicity we shall take to consist of five persons only) is 6-6-4-4-4. Now an invention comes along which will enormously increase the standard of living, so that the resulting distribution becomes 50-50-40-40-3. Would it be justified? No, presumably the invention would have to be suppressed in spite of the great rise in the standard of living of almost everyone, because one person in the society is slightly worse off because of it.[11]

The example Hospers gives to complete his argument is the invention of the automobile. The introduction of the automobile provided thousands of new jobs, made millions happy because they could travel farther and faster at a reasonable cost. Everyone was better off "except the manufacturer of buggy-whips, who once did a land-office business but is now out of work because of the new invention."[12] Not even the money the former manufacturer of buggy-whips might receive on welfare can begin to compensate for what he lost by the invention of the automobile. No matter how much better off everyone else

---

10. The argument is adapted from Brian Barry, *The Liberal Theory of Justice* (Oxford: Clarendon Press, 1973) pp. 16-17.
11. Hospers, *The Freeman*, op. cit., p. 755.
12. Ibid.

is, this one person has been disadvantaged. Would Rawls prohibit the invention? Since his second principle rules out inequalities that fail to work to the advantage of everyone, Hospers argues, "No major innovation would ever have occurred, from the dawn of history to the present, no matter how great its benefit to mankind," since there would always be "someone somewhere who [would be] worse off because of it."[13] It is evident that Rawls' system requires major alterations.

NOZICK'S LIBERTARIAN ANALYSIS OF JUSTICE

Nozick's book challenges theories of justice that require too great a dependence on the machinery of the state. Statists insist that a minimal state is impotent to deal with most problems of distributive justice. But in Nozick's view, "The minimal state is the most extensive state that can be justified. Any state more extensive violates people's rights."[14] Any attempt to justify a more extensive state in order to attain social justice is unfounded and dangerous. The attainment of justice does not require the existence of a super-state.

One of the more important advances in understanding the concept of justice that comes out of Nozick's book is the distinction he draws between *end-result* and *historical theories* of justice. End-result theories are *forward-looking* in the sense"that the justice of a distribution is determined by how things are distributed (who has what) as judged by some structural principle(s) of just distribution."[15] Historical approaches to justice look *backwards.* They "hold that past circumstances or actions of people can create differential entitlements or differential deserts to things."[16] For Nozick who advocates the historical approach, justice does not depend on some social

13. Ibid.
14. Nozick, op. cit., p. 149.
15. Ibid., p. 154.
16. Ibid., p. 155.

arrangement having consequences of a certain kind. Justice is tied rather to past and present considerations.

Nozick focuses his attention on one major representative of the end-result and the historical approaches to justice. He notes that many end-result theories attempt to locate justice in some pattern of distribution.

> Proponents of patterned principles of distributive justice focus upon criteria for determining who is to receive holdings; they consider the reasons for which someone should have something, and also the total picture of holdings. Whether or not it is better to give than to receive, proponents of patterned principles ignore giving altogether. In considering the distribution of goods, income, and so forth, their theories are theories of recipient justice; they completely ignore any right a person might have to give something to someone. . . . Patterned principles of distributive justice necessitate redistributive activities. The likelihood is small that any actual freely-arrived-at set of holdings fits a given pattern; and the likelihood is nil that it will continue to fit the pattern as people exchange and give.[17]

According to this view, if a particular distribution matches a preconceived pattern (and there are several possible patterns that might be adopted), then it is just. It makes no difference who the recipients are; nor does it matter if that which they receive is due them. All that counts is that the actual distribution fit the pattern. For example, egalitarians approach questions of justice with the assumption that a just distribution will tend toward a pattern of equality. When a political liberal talks about distributive justice on a societal level, he usually has three things in mind. First, he believes his society's present distribution is unjust because it fails to measure up to his preconceived pattern of how goods and burdens ought to be distributed. Secondly, he believes the present spread must be altered to match better his criterion. And finally, the required redistribution cannot be voluntary. Because the more privileged members of society will not willingly part with their greater share, the

17. Ibid., p. 168.

liberal wants the state to be authorized to take by force whatever the central authority believes necessary to meet the requirements of "justice." That this appropriation is normally effected through taxation does not, of course, alter the fact that it is an act of force.

Nozick's own proposal, a type of historical approach to justice, is called The Entitlement Theory of Justice. Nozick believes that pattern theories ignore ethically relevant factors in the past history of how people came to their present holdings, factors that are pertinent to what each person is due. Nozick urges that little attention be paid to the final pattern of distribution. What marks the holdings of people as just or unjust is not who holds what, but *how* each person acquired his holdings through a process of original acquisition and transfer. If a person is entitled to his holdings because its original acquisition was just and because the subsequent transfer that led to his holding were just, then he and others like him are entitled to their holdings and the distribution is just regardless of its pattern. Nozick distinguishes between a person's being entitled to a holding and deserving that holding. A person might have inherited money which he did not deserve. But his lack of desert does not weaken the fact that he is entitled to his wealth.

Two of Nozick's criticisms of pattern theories of justice will be noted. First, such attempts rest upon a misleading analogy. Distributive justice is a meaningful concept in many commonly encountered situations. Several examples were mentioned earlier: the decision confronting a parent about to divide the evening dessert within a family where the members differ considerably in size, age, needs, and hunger; a testator preparing his will; a university administrator who has x number of dollars to divide among a group of faculty as their raises for the next year.

Such paradigm cases have certain features in common. They are *controlled situations* in the sense that they are fairly limited in size and scope. The distributors have some legitimate claim to that which they are distributing and can usually, at least in principle, obtain the relevant information needed to come to a decision. For example, the parent about to divide the pie can ask how hungry everyone is. In such controlled everyday situations, the concept of distributive justice makes perfectly good sense.

However, a massive leap is required to get from the limited and controlled situations where considerations of distributive justice are obviously relevant to the unlimited and *spontaneous situations* found in society as a whole. In limited situations, justice is possible because the distributor usually has access to the information he needs to make his decisions. But when the context becomes as broad as an entire society, no one person or central authority can ever attain sufficient knowledge about the millions of individuals and the incalculable number of decisions, actions, and exchanges that have brought them to their present holdings. The more complex a society, the less likely it is that any one person or central agency can possess all the essential information. When the whole of society is in view, Nozick contends,

> . . . we are not in the position of children who have been given portions of pie by someone who now makes last minute adjustments to rectify careless cutting. There is no *central* distribution, no person or group entitled to control all the resources, jointly deciding how they are to be doled out. What each person gets, he gets from others who give to him in exchange for something, or as a gift. In a free society, diverse persons control different resources, and new holdings arise out of the voluntary exchanges and actions of persons. . . . The total result is the product of many individual decisions which the different individuals involved are entitled to make.[18]

The analogy between the limited situations in which distributive justice makes sense and the unlimited spontaneous situation that characterizes society as a whole is misleading for two reasons: first, because sufficient information in the case of a whole society is unattainable; and secondly, because no central

18. Ibid., pp. 149-150.

authority really has a right to the things it usually distributes.
As one of Nozick's commentators explains,

> Resources, Nozick insists, are not manna from heaven, requir-
> ing to be distributed by some person or group entitled to control
> the distribution; they are already distributed as a result of many
> individual transactions in the past, just or unjust. The assump-
> tion that there is a problem of distribution is the fundamental
> mistake of all theories of justice whose basic concern is to deter-
> mine 'who ends up with what.'[19]

Nozick's first objection to pattern theories of justice, then, is
the claim that their appeal to social justice is based upon a false
analogy between a just distribution in a limited controlled situation and a just distribution in an unlimited spontaneous
situation.

Nozick's second objection is that pattern theories are incompatible with freedom. This can easily be seen by imagining a
society marked by four conditions: (1) Assume that any one of
the several popular patterns of distributive justice has been successfully imposed on an entire society. For our purposes, it does
not matter which particular pattern it is. It might be a pattern
of equal distribution (whatever that should turn out to mean)
or distribution according to need; or any other theory. (2)
Suppose that the citizens are free to exchange or transfer their
holdings in any way they choose. (3) Assume that any appropriation of another person's holdings by theft, force, fraud or other
criminal activity will be recognized as unjust and forbidden by
law. (4) Finally, in order to eliminate an essentially irrelevant
objection, assume that this society contains no persons who are
unable to produce or exchange. Therefore, in any society where
our conditions are met, any noncriminal voluntary transfer or
exchange of holdings like property or money will be a just
transfer. That is, if we assume that the original holdings of
everyone in the initial situation (the situation obtained
immediately after the patterned distribution) are just because

19. B. J. Diggs, "Liberty Without Fraternity," *Ethics*, Vol. 87 (1977) p. 105.

they match the preconceived pattern of distributive justice, and if all subsequent transfers are just, then any deviation from the original pattern of holdings will be just, no matter how much it departs from the original pattern.[20] In any free society, it would not take long for new holdings to vary greatly from the original pattern of distribution. This situation would confront the defenders of that original pattern with three options.

(1) They might be sensible and realize that even though great discrepancies in holdings now exist, the disparity resulted from voluntary, legal, and just exchanges. And so even though the later situation no longer resembles the preferred pattern of distribution, the situation must be judged just and no further meddling with the new distribution is justified.

(2) What is more likely, given the mind-set of the ideologues, is that after a certain period of time, they would announce that the distribution is once again unacceptable, which fact would require the state to step in to rectify the situation. The use of words like "rectify" or "make right" in this context would certainly be odd since nothing immoral, criminal or unjust occurred. How can there be anything to rectify? The example makes it clear that appeals to rectification in such cases have little to do with justice or morality. The term simply provides another excuse for statist redistribution. But suppose, following the second establishment of the preferred pattern, that people are once again left free to do what they wish with their possessions. Similar deviations from the preferred pattern would soon reappear. And so the state would have to intervene again and again. Note that at the time of each redistribution, people who had acquired holdings honestly and fairly would be deprived of them without recourse; and this would be done in the name of justice.

(3) Should the state eventually grow tired of constantly forcing periodic redistributions, it could pursue the third possible course of action. It could simply deprive the citizens

20. In chapter seven of his book, Nozick supports this kind of reasoning with several ingenious examples that deserve careful study.

of the freedom to transfer and exchange their holdings at will.
That is, the state could intrude into the everyday affairs of each
citizen and control each and every action. As Nozick warns,

> . . . no end-state principle of justice can be continuously realized
> without continuous interference with people's lives. Any favored
> pattern would be transformed into one unfavored by the princi-
> ple, by people choosing to act in various ways; for example, by
> people exchanging goods and services with other people, or giving
> things to other people, things the transferrers are entitled to
> under the favored distributional pattern. To maintain a pattern
> one must either continually interfere to stop people from trans-
> ferring resources as they wish to, or continually (or periodically)
> interfere to take from some persons resources that others for
> some reason chose to transfer to them.[21]

Social justice, as viewed by statist proponents of pattern
approaches, is possible only in a society that is controlled from
the top down. There must be a central agency with the power
to force people to accept the preferred pattern of distribution.
And because people's normal desires will lead them to
exchanges that will upset the original pattern, the pattern can
only be preserved by continuous interference with the lives of
its citizens. If social justice is to have any meaning, any factors
that might contribute to spontaneous deviations from the
desired pattern must be eliminated. It is understandable how
Friedrich Hayek could speak of social justice as "the Trojan
Horse through which totalitarianism has entered many societies
in the world."[22]

The statist assumes that his promotion of social justice
simply means the addition of a new moral value to those known
in the past. He believes this new moral value "can be fitted
within the existing framework of moral rules. What is not
sufficiently recognized is that in order to give [social justice]
meaning a complete change of the whole character of the social
order will have to be effected, and that some of the values which

21. Nozick, op. cit., p. 163.
22. Hayek, *Law* II, op. cit., p. 136.

used to govern it will have to be sacrificed." Hayek fears that "like most attempts to pursue an unattainable goal, the striving for [social justice] will also produce highly undesirable consequences, and in particular lead to the destruction of the indispensable environment in which the traditional moral values alone can flourish, namely personal freedom."[23]

ADDITIONAL DIMENSIONS OF JUSTICE

To this point, the discussion of Nozick's theory of justice has focused on his view of what is called *justice in transfer*, that is, under what conditions is a transfer of holdings just? Nozick correctly recognizes that any adequate theory of justice must address two additional problems that he calls *justice in original acquisition* and *justice in rectification*. The technical terminology shouldn't be allowed to obscure the importance of the topics.

One of the things Nozick is saying is that a person's holdings are just if the exchange process by which he obtained those holdings was just. If person B buys something from person A at a market price, the transfer is just. If B steals that thing from A or obtains it by force or fraud, the transfer is unjust. But additional factors can complicate the justice of a person's holdings. Consider the following example.

Suppose I have gone fishing, caught a nice trout and then decide that I would rather sell the fish than eat it. Imagine that I sell the fish to Larry Mayhew for ten dollars. Suppose further that after Mayhew and I have exchanged the fish for his money, someone else challenges my ownership of the fish. If I caught the fish in public waters, it is unlikely that my original ownership of the fish could be challenged successfully. But suppose I caught the fish while trespassing on a farm owned by Arvin Vos. He might claim that since I had caught the fish illegally

23. Ibid., p. 67.

from his lake, my original acquisition of the fish was unjust. Even though my transfer of the fish seemed to be proper, the injustice of my original title to the fish tainted the exchange process. The justice of any exchange process presupposes that people have a legitimate title to that which they are exchanging.

The example could be extended even further by imagining that Mr. Vos insists that his fish be returned to him. But another problem now arises. Not only did Mr. Mayhew believe he had obtained rightful ownership of the fish, he had proceeded to eat the fish. Mr. Vos can no longer get his fish back. Mr. Vos raises the issue of *justice in rectification* and demands compensation for his stolen fish. Obviously Vos is justified in making this demand.

Nozick is certainly correct when he recognizes that the justice of a person's holdings depends upon more than the fact that he obtained those holdings through a fair exchange (justice in transfer). The person with whom he made the transfer must have had rightful title to what he traded. If somewhere along the trail of previous ownership, force, fraud or theft entered the picture, the ownership is negated and the question of rectification enters the picture.

In some cases, the laws regarding rectification are fairly clear. Take the case of a burglar who steals a valuable coin collection from Mr. A and then sells the collection to an innocent third party for $10,000. If the stolen collection is recognized, the innocent third party will not only lose the coin collection, he will also lose his money unless he can recover it from the thief. In other cases, justice in rectification can become very difficult to apply. To return to the earlier example of the fish caught on farmer Vos's property, imagine that the trespassing fisherman was a descendant of the Indian tribe that had originally lived on the land now owned by farmer Vos. Suppose the Indian defended his right to the fish he caught by arguing that the land in question had been unjustly appropriated from his ancestors generations before. Such a claim would introduce additional complications to the questions of original ownership and rectification. What justifies any person's first claim to original ownership of something like land? If people generations ago were deprived of their holdings unjustly, what rectification may be owed to their descendants by people who were not parties in the original injustice? The theoretical discussion necessary to identify and defend principles that can be used to settle such disputes obviously lies beyond the scope of this book. In countries like the United States, such cases will be settled in the courts. Each case should be tried on its merits. Where the decision of the courts seems unfair, concerned Christians should become involved either by lending their support to appeals to a higher court or by supporting changes in the law.

JUST RESULTS OR JUST PROCEDURES

Our study of the differences between patterned and entitlement theories of justice can help us see that one of the major differences between a liberal and conservative understanding of justice involves a choice between an approach that insists that the attainment of justice is impossible apart from the realization of certain just *results* and a competing view that maintains that a just society is one that adopts just *procedures*. A theory that places its emphasis upon just procedures will recognize that there is no way of specifying or knowing in advance what a just result would be. All one can do is try to make the procedures as just as possible. Then, whatever results from those just procedures must be recognized as just. One example often used in discussions of procedural justice is the case of gambling. Forgetting for the moment the moral questions gambling raises for some, if the gamblers keep the rules, if there is no cheating, then the result, whatever it turns out to be, is just. Obviously, a gambler victimized by loaded dice or a doped race horse or a bribed umpire can plead the injustice of the outcome. But if the procedures agreed to in advance are followed fairly, any loser's complaint about the injustice of his loss is empty rhetoric. Most conservatives believe that procedural justice is the model of justice most appropriate to a free economy and a free society. Even Rawls has kind things to say about it.

> Now the great practical advantage of pure procedural justice is that it is no longer necessary in meeting the demands of justice to keep track of the endless variety of circumstances and the changing relative positions of particular persons. One avoids the problem of defining principles to cope with the enormous complexities which would arise if such details were relevant. It is a mistake to focus attention on the varying relative positions of individuals and to require that every change, considered as a single transaction viewed in isolation, be in itself just. . . . A distribution cannot be judged in isolation from the system of which it is the outcome or from what individuals have done in good faith in the light of established expectations. If it is asked in the abstract whether one distribution of a given stock of things to definite individuals with known desires and preferences is better than another, then there is simply no answer to this question.[24]

Taken literally, this passage implies that even Rawls would shy away from the totalitarian implications of a patterned approach to justice.

The system of economic exchanges found in the free market is analogous to a kind of game. During the course of the game, much can be done to insure that the conduct of the players will be fair or just. The rules can be announced and enforced by impartial officials. But beyond seeing that the game is played fairly, nothing can or should be done to guarantee a "just" result, that is, a score that is morally satisfying to the spectator. One might feel that because one of the teams has lost fifty straight times that it "deserves" to win. But any cheating on the part of the players or favoritism on the part of the umpires that would help realize the "morally preferable" outcome would be unjust. Once the rules have been agreed upon in advance of play, any violation of those rules is an injustice.

24. Rawls, op. cit., pp. 87-88.

And if the game is played according to the rules, no one can complain that the final score is unjust. The liberal's confusion of economic and moral merit leads him to want to "fix" the final score.

While the analogy of the market to a game serves a useful purpose in illustrating the kind of procedural justice that should be stressed in a free society, the analogy probably should not be pushed too far. In the case of games, today's score seldom affects tomorrow's play. If the Cincinnati Reds beat the Los Angeles Dodgers 21-0 today, they both begin tomorrow's play dead even. Regrettably, the economic game does not work that way. The economic game, in a sense, seldom ends and there are many times when those who have lost remain losers indefinitely; and their losses may affect the ability of their offspring to play the game in the future. To be sure, proponents of the welfare state overstate this problem and ignore the countless thousands who have used the freedom and opportunity of the market to succeed in spite of great handicaps.

But what if the market, in spite of the advantages it has brought to the poor of past generations, is incapable of relieving all poverty and need? Should those unable to help themselves be allowed to suffer? If one were to ask a typical liberal, at this point, what he thought the conservative answer to this question would be, he would most likely suggest the conservative would say something like "Let them eat cake." It is not exactly clear how the false stereotype of the callous and heartless conservative grew to the proportions it presently occupies in liberal mythology. If one allows the conservative to speak for himself, an entirely different picture emerges. No twentieth century thinker is better known for his opposition to liberalism, collectivism and the welfare state than Friedrich Hayek. But Hayek is quite clear about his own conviction that a free society has an obligation to care for those who cannot care for themselves.

> There is no reason why in a free society government should not assure to all protection against severe deprivation in the form of an assured minimum income, or a floor below which nobody

need to descend. To enter into such an insurance against extreme misfortune may well be in the interest of all; or it may be felt to be a clear moral duty of all to assist, within the organized community, those who cannot help themselves. So long as such a uniform minimum income is provided outside the market to all those who, for any reason, are unable to earn in the market an adequate maintenance, this need not lead to a restriction of freedom, or conflict with the Rule of Law. The problems with which we are here concerned arise only when the remuneration for services rendered is determined by authority, and the impersonal mechanism of the market which guides the direction of individual efforts is thus suspended.[25]

The alleviation of suffering in an affluent society can occur through extra-market means that fall far short of granting the state the added powers statists believe it must have. Details of several ways in which this might be done can be derived from such works as Hayek's *The Constitution of Liberty* and Milton Friedman's *Capitalism and Freedom* or his more recent work, *Free to Choose.*

ECONOMIC MERIT AND MORAL MERIT

Questions of distributive justice could never arise apart from some economic system within which scarce goods can be acquired and exchanged. The economic system produces the pie; it is quite another thing to provide criteria to determine the most just way to cut the pie. Economics itself does not provide the criteria of a just distribution. Economics *qua* economics deals with the means by which certain ends can be realized; it does not pass judgment on the morality of those ends. Obviously, individual economists make moral judgments all the time. But the market itself does not presume to place any value on human choices. That is the task of moral philosophy and theology which serve as indispensable helpmates for economics. The market provides incentives for people to produce and makes

25. Hayek, *Law* II, op. cit., p. 87.

it possible for them to transfer and exchange their holdings. What transpires in the market will be as moral or immoral as the human beings who are active in the market. The moral criteria that judge those actions and their consequences must come from some discipline other than economics. Because the market itself is amoral and does not supply the moral standards to evaluate what transpires within the system, it is a mistake to confuse *economic merit* (the value something has in the market) with *moral merit*. Just because a well-known athlete commands a yearly salary of $750,000, it does not follow that he possesses more moral merit than a poorly paid minister or nurse. What people deserve economically and morally are not the same. There may be good economic reasons for paying a skilled baseball player twenty or thirty times as much as a skilled philosophy teacher, even though the philosopher may be more deserving in a moral sense. The widespread tendency to connect moral and economic merit ought to be avoided. Because many people are offended by the fact that someone who is less deserving in a moral sense is worth more economically, they believe steps should be taken to alter the situation through statist action. It is worth noting that there never seem to be enough people willing to alter the situation economically, for example, by paying more to hear the philosopher lecture than to watch the athlete perform.

The socialist attempt to apply moral principles to economic activities leads to a confusion of moral and economic desert. The socialist wishes to replace the market where value depends upon supply and demand with a socio-economic system which rewards moral merit. It is not difficult to organize dissatisfaction with the actual distribution of the market. It is natural to feel moral outrage at the prosperity of the wicked; it is easy to feel envy at the prosperity of the righteous. As long as some have more than others, it is natural for discontent to arise among those with less. But those who believe that statist interference with the market will guarantee the primacy of moral merit are mistaken. Once the distribution is placed in the hands of the state or any other centralized authority, it is highly likely that moral merit will once again be reduced to second place while the major shares go to reward political merit, which is exactly what one finds in Marxist states. The attempt to alleviate the disparities resulting from the market's reward of economic merit could lead to a highly discriminatory and politically biased distribution that is just as much in conflict with a moral perspective. Instead of being rewarded for economic contributions or for moral merit, a person will be rewarded for service to the state.

CONCLUSION

The liberal preference for patterned theories of justice raises great difficulties, especially for any society that hopes to remain free. We have noted an alternative approach that places its emphasis not upon just results (which can never be guaranteed) but upon just procedures. A society which follows just procedures is certainly just in this one respectable sense of the word. To those who complain that such a society still produces "unjust" results, two replies are relevant. We agree that an emphasis on procedural justice will sometimes produce results that are unpleasant or unsatisfactory. In cases where this means that people will suffer unfairly as a result of correctable problems, the advocates of procedural justice have repeatedly recommended actions that would help those who cannot help themselves. But it is not self-evident that words like "injustice" are used appropriately when describing the unpleasant results that bother so many. In most cases, it seems, words like "injustice" are thrown carelessly around as labels for whatever some people find personally or morally unsatisfactory. Such claims often involve a careless confusion between what people deserve morally and what they deserve economically.

Chapter Five

Justice and the Welfare State

Given the liberal's conviction that social justice is inseparable from a state-enforced redistribution of people's holdings, the rise of the modern welfare state is understandable. It is interesting to note, however, that no adequate justification for the welfare state has yet been given. This fact is openly acknowledged by the authors of a recent book defending the welfare state. They admit that "The social philosophy behind the welfare state is vague and inchoate."[1] The highly regarded American philosopher, Sidney Hook, concedes that "the absence of a dominant theorist or of a single commanding system of thought endorsing the welfare state has been documented again and again."[2] Even though a plausible case for the welfare state has yet to be made, its supporters contend that the welfare state must be continued because it, more than any rival view of government, "conforms to the elemental standards of justice and decency."[3] Once again, we find an appeal to an undefined notion of justice. Obviously, the given reason does not exactly constitute indisputable evidence.

Several considerations weigh heavily against the welfare state. Attention has already been drawn to such matters as the welfare state's threat to personal liberty. Donald J. Devine notes some of these other problems.

1. Norman Furniss and Timothy Tilton, *The Case for the Welfare State* (Bloomington, In.: Indiana University Press, 1977) p. 23.

2. Sidney Hook, " 'Welfare State'—a Debate that Isn't," in *The Welfare State*, ed. E.I. Schottland (New York: Harper and Row, 1967) p. 167.

3. Furniss, op. cit.

Beyond the problem of whether real welfare is provided and whether this reaches those who deserve it, is the fundamental problem that coercion, including government coercion, can cause injury which is typically feared as the worst injustice which can be inflicted upon a society. Government injury may be done to those who are forced to contribute so that others may have goods or services, or to those who are forced to behave in a certain manner so that others may have a congenial environment and social companionship.[4]

Evidence exists that welfare state policies do more than injure those from whom something is *taken*; they also injure those to whom something is *given* (by the state). Liberal housing programs did not make more low-cost housing available for the poor; the result has been much less available housing, at a cost of billions of dollars. Minimum wage legislation does not really help people at the bottom of the economic ladder; it ends up harming them by making them less employable, thus increasing unemployment among the very people the legislation is supposed to help. The short-sighted and politically expedient policy of paying for social welfare through deficit government spending has flooded the economy with billions of dollars of increasingly worthless money and ravaged the poor by subjecting them (and everyone else) to an inflation that continues to raise the prices of basic necessities beyond their reach. Regardless of where one looks, welfare state programs have failed. Liberal social policies have done the most harm in basic areas like food and clothing. The people who have been hurt the most have been those least able to afford it, the very people, the liberal assures us, he is trying to help.[5]

Of course, claims like these run contrary to the tide of contemporary political "wisdom." Advocates of the welfare state argue that if their efforts have fallen short of their humanitarian goals, it is because obstinate apologists for the status quo kept

4. Donald J. Devine, "Welfare Without Injustice," *Modern Age*, 1977, p. 161.

5. Those interested in a powerful, documented indictment of the counter-productiveness of liberal social action should consult M. Stanton Evans, *Clear and Present Dangers* (New York: Harcourt, Brace, Jovanovich, 1975).

the liberal state from attaining all of the powers it needed. In spite of all the power concentrated in the state and in spite of all the liberal failures, these miscarriages are offered as reasons for giving the state even greater influence, rather than as evidence for calling the liberal view into question.

It is not a lack of compassion that leads the conservative to oppose the welfare state. On the contrary, it is his compassion plus a decidedly clearer vision of the consequences of welfare state policies that produces his opposition. George Gilder has received much attention of late for his thesis that liberalism has turned out to be an enemy of the poor while conservatism advances principles that end up working to the best advantage of the poor. In his view, conservatives "have become the best friends of the poor in America, while liberalism administers new forms of bondage and new fashions of moral corruption to poor families."[6] Gilder goes so far as to write of the "overall moral hazard of the welfare state."[7] Liberals who write such glowing reports of all the progress the American poor have made in their struggle against poverty since the alleged beginnings of the war on poverty in 1964 have, Gilder argues, a badly distorted vision of reality.

> What actually happened since 1964 was a vast expansion of the welfare rolls that halted in its tracks an ongoing improvement in the lives of the poor, particularly blacks, and left behind— and here I choose my words as carefully as I can—a wreckage of broken lives and families worse than the aftermath of slavery. Although intact black families are doing better than ever, and discrimination has vastly diminished, the condition of poor blacks has radically worsened."[8]

It is not as though the liberal welfare state has not thrown enough money at the problems. Walter Williams, a black economist, points out that the cumulative total spent at every

6. George Gilder, *Wealth and Poverty* (New York: Basic Books, 1981) pp. xi-xii.
7. Ibid., p. 111.
8. Ibid., chapter one.

level of government in the United States just to fight poverty is $250 billion a year.[9] If this amount of money were given equally to all the families below the poverty level, each one would receive an annual payment of $34,000. The obvious reason why this amount never reaches the poor is the massive bureaucratic system that has grown up with the welfare state and which siphons off most of the money.[10] According to Gilder,

> The figures indicate that the average welfare family of four received about $15,000 worth of subsidies in 1976 and close to $18,000 worth in 1979. These totals, which are real averages, not extreme cases, compare with an American median income of approximately $14,500 in 1976 and $16,500 in 1979, and annual minimum-wage earnings and benefits of about half the welfare level.[11]

Another black economist, Thomas Sowell, states: "The amount necessary to lift every man, woman and child in America above the poverty line has been calculated, and it is one-third of what is in fact spent on poverty programs. Clearly, much of the transfer ends up in the pockets of highly paid administrators, consultants, and staff as well as higher-income recipients of benefits from programs advertised as anti-poverty efforts."[12] Surely the bucket used to carry money from the pockets of the taxpayer to the poor is leaking badly. Many think the real beneficiaries of liberal social programs are not the poor and disadvantaged but the members of the governmental bureaucracy who administer the programs. One should not impugn the motives of all who call themselves liberals. But

9. Walter E. Williams, "Commentary," *Newsweek*, Sept. 24, 1979, pp. 57-59. The reader should also consult Thomas Sowell, *Race and Economics* (New York: David McKay, 1975) pp. 195-200.

10. Worth reading in this regard are the following: Tom Bethell, "The Wealth of Washington," *Harpers*, June 1, 1978, pp. 41-60 and Tom Alexander, "Why Bureaucracy Keeps Growing," *Fortune*, May 7, 1979.

11. Gilder, op. cit., pp. 111-112; for verification of these figures, see Charles D. Hobbs, *The Welfare Industry* (Washington, D.C.: The Heritage Foundation, 1978) pp. 83, 84.

12. Thomas Sowell, "The Uses of Government for Racial Equality," *National Review*, Sept. 4, 1981, p. 1013.

neither should one overlook the fact that the army of bureaucrats whose business is "helping the poor" are doing considerably better than those they're supposed to be helping. M. Stanton Evans charges:

> The principal beneficiaries of the money absorbed and dispensed by government are not poor blacks in ghettos or Appalachian whites or elderly pensioners receiving Social Security checks— the usual figures conjured up when social welfare is discussed. The major beneficiaries, instead, are the *employees of government itself*—people engaged in administering some real or imagined service to the underprivileged or, as the case may be, the overprivileged. . . . The gross effect of increased government spending is to transfer money away from relatively low income people—average taxpayers who must pay the bills—to relatively high income people—Federal functionaries who are being paid out of the taxpayer's pocket.[13]

As Evans notes further, "the two richest counties in the United States are . . . Montgomery County, Maryland, and Fairfax County, Virginia—principal bedroom counties for Federal workers in Washington, D.C."[14] Evans shows that it pays to serve the poor under the aegis of the liberal welfare state.

Liberals and conservatives also disagree over the identification of the truly needy. Obviously, our country contains many unfortunate children and adults who face insurmountable medical bills, who are unable to work or who cannot find work, who cannot help themselves. But liberal social programs benefit large numbers of people who can be regarded as "needy" only in a grossly extended sense of the word. Do middle class college students really have a *right* to subsidized loans or food stamps? Moreover, liberal social programs have often been so shortsighted and so poorly designed that they have resulted in large numbers of people becoming slavishly dependent on the state. Liberal social programs can be compared to heroin addiction. Once dependence is established, the continual supply of what

13. M. Stanton Evans, *Clear and Present Dangers*, op. cit., p. 127.
14. Ibid., pp. 127-128.

was supposed to be a temporary palliation becomes a matter of life and death. People come to view the temporary dole as their never-ending right.

The liberal's obsession with the proper distribution of society's goods blinds him to a crucial truth: that before society can have enough to distribute among the needy, a sufficient quantity of goods must be *produced.* By focusing all their attention on who gets what, defenders of the welfare state promote policies that severely restrict production. Advocates of the welfare state paint a picture of an unending flow of cash from the producers in society to the nonproducers. But as the sphere of benefits for the nonproductive segment of society continues to increase, the mass of marginal producers realizes that the gap between them and welfare recipients is shrinking. Inevitably, they begin to lose their incentive to continue as producers—and as taxpayers. So they give up and join the evergrowing army drawing welfare benefits paid for by the diminishing group of producers. Liberal social policies that continue to drain a society's productive capacities hold ominous implications for the welfare of future generations. This is already apparent in the case of the social security system. A genuine concern for the welfare of future generations should result in economic policies that will encourage a thriving productive base that will allow future generations to meet their own needs and permit them the luxury of supporting their contemporaries who may suffer from deprivation.

One proponent of the welfare state has fairly and accurately articulated a separate concern of many who oppose the system:

> Many people believe that nearly all welfare programs . . . reward the irresponsible and self-indulgent and penalize the frugal and self-sufficient. For example, it is argued that self-sufficient middle-class people tend to postpone gratification and hence sacrifice today for greater benefits tomorrow. Middle-class children defer immediate income from jobs to attend college. They also defer marriage and the starting of a family until after college. It is further widely believed that middle-class families limit the number of children they have while lower-class poor families do

not. . . . These middle-class taxpayers who pay the welfare bills then feel aggrieved because they believe they are being penalized for limiting the number of children they have. They are responsible enough to limit the number of their children to those they can support, and yet they are also being taxed to pay for children on welfare.[15]

It does seem to require a strong dose of ideology to call such discrimination justice. The Equal Education Opportunity Act is a perfect illustration of such discrimination. Consider two families with identical incomes for several years. Suppose one family made numerous sacrifices in order to acquire savings and a financial security that would give their children a college education. Assume that the other family, with the same income, failed to practice the conservative measures of the first family. While it could have saved as much as the first, it spent excess funds on expensive vacations and fancy cars. How does the welfare state reward the sacrifices of the first family and the extravagances of the second? It does so by awarding the children of the second family scholarships it denies to the first. Is this liberal justice in action?

Norman Bowie continues:

A second cause of resentment is captured by the notion of the culture of poverty. It is argued that once a person is on welfare, he or she seems content to stay there. Indeed the children of persons on welfare seem to end up on welfare too. . . . Welfare payments to families, it is argued, are simply a waste. Give them money and it goes for booze. Give them a decent home and it will soon be a wreck. Welfare recipients have neither the intellectual ability nor the moral character to use income, food stamps, or low-income housing as opportunities to get their feet on the ground and out of poverty. As a result, welfare recipients are not entitled to a minimum standard of living, and society has no obligation to provide it, indeed, most of the tax money used for welfare is simply wasted.[16]

15. Norman E. Bowie, "Welfare and Freedom," *Ethics*, 1979, pp. 261-262.
16. Ibid., p. 262. Further points along these lines are made by Edward Banfield in his book, *The Unheavenly City* (Boston: Little, Brown & Co., 1968).

Bowie, it must be remembered, supports the welfare state and is summarizing what he takes to be the basis for resentment against the system. He does a good job. Nor can he deny some truth in these allegations. Bowie counters by arguing that the last objection ignores important distinctions within the class of poor people. Some people are poor for reasons beyond their control or responsibility. They may have been victimized by illness or some handicap; they may have been orphaned or widowed; their parents may have failed them; they may have become unemployed through no fault of their own. The point is, some poor people do have ambition and lack only some assistance to move beyond poverty. Bowie is right; many of the poor can be helped and should be helped.

Bowie notes a second class of the poor that presents more difficulties. This is the group of the unmotivated poor. In spite of this group's bad attitudes and the fact that they appear not to care, the availability of new opportunities might produce a change of attitudes in some of them. Thus, while all the members of the first class of poor people might respond favorably to welfare, only a percentage of the second group will ever be truly helped.

The third and final class of the poor is that group which, Bowie acknowledges, is hopeless. Regardless of what the state does for them, they will never improve. Bowie admits that middle-class resentment appears justified in the case of this third group. But, he argues, there is no way of knowing for sure what percentage of the poor belongs to the irredeemable group. Nor is there agreement on the justifiable extent to which the middle-class taxpayer should be forced to sacrifice to reach the uncertain percentage in class two that can be helped.

Some conservatives like Milton Friedman have urged the adoption of welfare proposals that retain an important place for incentives. The individual on welfare should be encouraged, and not discouraged, to find employment and move off the welfare rolls. Anti-statist measures would restrict drastically the size of the bureaucracy required to dispense the welfare and reduce the amount of statist intervention into the everyday lives of every citizen, taxpayer and welfare recipient. Conservatives have, for years, urged an end to the myriad of programs presently in existence in favor of the adoption of one simple and far more cost-effective means of transferring money from one group to another. This means is a negative income tax, which should not be confused with the parody discussed during the Nixon presidency. Once in place, the negative income tax would eliminate the need for much of the massive welfare bureaucracy presently in place; it would transfer funds directly to the poor; and would give real incentives to those able to work to terminate their slavish dependence on the state. Repeated liberal rejection of such a measure coupled with the repeated failures of their own programs suggest that the liberal's real concerns lie in directions other than providing help for the needy. With increasing frequency, one hears the suggestion that liberal programs are necessary to the statist, not as a means of aiding the poor, but as a means to the statist's possession of power; and that, many believe, is what the liberal state is all about. It is ironic then that politically liberal Christians who sincerely wish to help the poor end up supporting policies that actually benefit the members of the Federal establishment. The belief that the welfare state is an indispensable means to social justice is a myth whose time has passed.

Chapter Six

Justice and the Bible

One interesting feature of the current infatuation with
statism is the affection with which it is held by many Christian clergymen. Friedrich Hayek is struck by the fact that much
of the current interest in social justice occurs in clergymen
"who, while increasingly losing their faith in a supernatural
revelation, appear to have sought a refuge and consolation in
a new 'social' religion which substitutes a temporal for a
celestial promise of justice, and who hope that they can thus
continue their striving to do good."[1] Several theologically liberal
Christian organizations have, for example, made large donations
in the name of social justice to terrorist groups in Africa and
Latin America. Liberal social activists who are theologically
conservative have not yet done anything this extreme. But as
we have seen, they do believe that the Christian's social responsibility obliges him to adopt liberal and statist means to aid
the poor and some even cast aspersions about the genuineness
of a religious commitment that does not openly embrace a
statist approach to social justice. In this chapter, we will
examine the efforts of such thinkers to find support for their
position in the Bible.

The notion of justice appears frequently in the Scriptures.
But as the previous argument has suggested, the word "justice"
has a variety of meanings. It is disconcerting to see someone
quote a biblical text containing the word "justice," ignore all

1. Friedrich Hayek, *Law, Legislation and Liberty* II, op. cit., p. 66.

questions about the particular meaning the term has in that context, and simply presume that the verse functions as a proof-text for his position. For example, some of these verses refer not to distributive justice but to remedial justice. This is clearly true in the case of Exodus 23:6 which warns against depriving the poor man of justice but makes it obvious that the justice in view is that found in a court of law. The same chapter (Ex. 23:3) also warns against showing partiality toward the poor in a court of law.

One recurring error in many attempts to support a particular ideology with biblical texts that mention justice is the failure to distinguish between the *interpretation* of a verse and its *application*. The writings of liberation theologians and evangelical social activists should be studied carefully with this claim in mind. Anxious to make their point, such writers often quote a particular passage and jump immediately to what they regard as the self-evident application, completely skipping in the process important questions about the interpretation of the text. A good example of this is an article by Eric Beversluis in *Christian Scholar's Review.*[2] Beversluis quotes Exodus 22:26-27 which states that if a neighbor has turned over his cloak as collateral for a loan and if that neighbor has no other way to protect himself from the cold, then the person holding the cloak should make it available during times when it is needed. The interpretation of the passage poses no special problems but Beversluis leaps at once to his application: "A person has a right to the material goods she or he needs for a decent existence. Thus the Bible teaches that there are rights to specific kinds of economic goods, and that these rights bind governments as well as individuals."[3] Most readers of this article will be surprised at the ease with which Beversluis gets all this from those two simple verses. Many will conclude, with some justification, that he simply reads his position into the

2. Eric Beversluis, "Christianity, Economic Justice and the State," *Christian Scholar's Review*, fall, 1982.
3. Ibid.

texts. Obviously, whatever he is doing, it is not exegesis.

The most obvious application of Exodus 22:26-27 suggests that if a person loans money and the borrower assigns as collateral for the loan something that he subsequently needs to meet some temporary emergency, then the lender has an obligation not to withhold that which he needs. But what does Beversluis extract from the text? Before one knows it, he has used the passage to support a theory of state-enforced economic redistribution. While it may be true that people have economic rights that bind governments, that doctrine cannot be found in Exodus 22:26-27.

As stated, one important hermeneutical principle commonly ignored by Christian social activists is the distinction between interpretation and application. Another principle that gets short-changed in their treatment of Scripture is the importance of reading a passage in the light of its context. Beversluis does not say anything in his article about the other verses in Exodus 22; his silence is understandable. Since the entire chapter contains a large number of other injunctions, it is interesting to speculate how many of them should also be sanctioned by Beversluis' government. Exodus 22:18-20 is a good example. If Beversluis handled these three verses in the same way he treats verses 26-27, his contemporary state would be obliged to execute witches, sex perverts and idolaters. As Jacob Petuchowski of Hebrew-Union College pointed out several years ago:

> It becomes a matter of biblical exegesis and hermeneutics to determine whether or not the biblical texts, originally addressed to a primitive agrarian society, really commit the latter-day believer to an espousal of socialism in the modern world. . . . Still it is quite possible to produce one-sided and partisan collections of biblical and rabbinic proof-texts which would clearly demonstrate that religion commits us to this or that political program or social action platform.[4]

4. Jacob J. Petuchowski, "The Altar Throne Clash Updated," *Christianity Today*, Sept. 23, 1977, pp. 20ff.

Much of the confusion present in evangelical attempts to find a theory of distributive justice in the Bible results from inattention to the classical distinction between a universal and particular sense of justice. Because evangelical social liberals are inattentive to important distinctions within the notion of justice, many of their appeals to biblical uses of "justice" are compromised since they simply assume that biblical endorsements of justice are divine commands to support economic redistribution. This kind of error is illustrated in Robert Johnston's book, *Evangelicals at an Impasse.* Johnston writes:

> Although it is not the Bible's purpose to give a careful scientific definition of what our 'needs' are, Scripture does repeatedly identify justice with asssistance for the poor, the sick, and the powerless. Job states, for example:

> I put on righteousness, and it clothed me;
> 　　my justice was like a robe and a turban.
> I was eyes to the blind,
> 　　and feet to the lame.
> I was a father to the poor,
> 　　and I searched out the cause of him
> 　　whom I did not know.
> I broke the fangs of the unrighteous, and
> 　　made him drop his prey from his teeth.[5]

Johnston goes on to cite several other texts where the notion of justice is conjoined with helping the poor (Jer. 22:15-16; Deut. 10:12-22; Ps. 103:6; Ps. 146:7-9). Such verses prove, in Johnston's judgment, that biblical justice is closely related to an economic redistribution that will meet the needs of the poor and the helpless.

It is certainly not the intent of this book to challenge the belief that God cares for the poor and helpless. The question at this

---

5. Robert K. Johnston, *Evangelicals at an Impasse* (Atlanta: John Knox Press, 1979) p. 99. The Job text is from the New International Version translation of Job 29:14-17.

point is whether Johnston and other evangelical liberals are interpreting Scripture correctly. In this case, it seems that they are not. Is Job 29:14-17 an endorsement of the kind of coercive redistribution of people's holdings that is essential to liberal statism? The obvious point to the text flows out of our earlier consideration of the distinction between universal and particular senses of justice. In that discussion, we pointed out that "justice" was frequently used in classical times as a synonym for personal righteousness. In that universal sense, justice did indeed entail a possession of all the other major virtues *including* helping the poor. It is not surprising that Scripture repeatedly mentions justice in contexts that also refer to love, to helping the poor, and to giving food to the hungry. But are these biblical appeals to justice discussions of the kind of universal justice that is synonymous with personal righteousness or are they references to a particular theory of distributive justice? Obviously, they are the former. What the Job text teaches is that God expects every truly righteous person to care about the poor and to do what is in his power to help them. But it begs the question to maintain that this concern can only be expressed in an endorsement of the coercive and redistributory statism that is so essential to contemporary collectivist approaches to justice. Evangelical liberals therefore ignore the several different senses of "justice" and simply assume that the kind of justice mentioned in their proof-texts is distributive justice.

The line of argument against Robert Johnston's proof-texts[6] has been criticized by Eric Beversluis. Beversluis thinks he discovers a fatal flaw in the argument by suggesting that particular justice is really only a species of universal justice. It deserves careful consideration. To review the earlier discussion,

6. It should be noted that Johnston's procedure is similar to that found in the writings of several liberation theologians as well as to that taken by Stephen Charles Mott in his paper, "Egalitarian Aspects of the Biblical Theory of Justice," published in *Selected Papers of the American Society of Christian Ethics*, 1978.

we used Aristotle's discussion of justice as a starting point and distinguished among the following types of justice:

UNIVERSAL JUSTICE   PARTICULAR JUSTICE

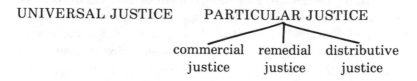

commercial   remedial   distributive
justice   justice   justice

While the word "justice" is seldom used in Aristotle's universal sense anymore, this usage was very common in the ancient world. Plato said much about it in his *Republic* and, of course, it appears prominently in the Bible. Universal justice is synonymous with personal righteousness and might be called *justice as virtue*. When the Bible says that Noah was a just man, it doesn't mean he voted the straight Democratic ticket; it simply means he was a virtuous man. Particular justice is especially concerned with fairness. The man or woman who is just in Aristotle's particular sense does not seek more than his fair share. We could characterize particular justice as *justice as fairness*. Fairness comes into play in many areas of life. Identifying three contexts where particular justice is especially important, Aristotle referred to commercial, remedial and distributive justice, namely justice in economic exchanges, in courts of law, and in situations where some good or burden is to be distributed between two or more people.

Two questions must now be asked. (1) What is the relationship between particular justice on the one hand and, on the other, commercial, remedial and distributive justice? The answer is obvious. All three are species of particular justice. Particular justice means treating people fairly. Commercial, remedial and distributive justice are three different settings in which the question of fair treatment arises.

(2) But what is the relationship between universal and particular justice? Beversluis simply assumes that particular justice is a species of universal justice. This leads him to write: "Clearly the particular virtue of justice . . . is *part of* universal

justice. . . . But then if the Bible mandates universal justice, it thereby mandates its parts, including distributive (economic) justice."[7] Perhaps Beversluis got confused by Aristotle's labels. It might be easy to suppose that Aristotle called one kind of justice "particular justice" because he viewed it as a part of universal justice. But the supposition is mistaken. Universal justice is universal because it is a kind of justice that can be practiced by all human beings; it is not necessary for a person to occupy a particular role or be in a particular situation in order to be personally righteous. One can be just in Aristotle's universal sense whether or not he is a businessman or a judge or someone charged with the responsibility of distributing some good. Universal justice is universal because we normally hope to find this justice present in every human being; it is supposed to be universal in scope. Being virtuous should not depend upon one's being in a particular type of situation. But particular justice is situational in the sense that people can practice these kinds of justice if and only if they are in a particular type of situation. A person can practice commercial justice if and only if he is involved in an economic exchange. A person can practice remedial justice if and only if he occupies one of several possible roles with regard to criminal or civil law. And a person can practice distributive justice if and only if he is in a situation where he is involved in the distribution of some good or some burden. The reason why commercial, remedial and distributive justice are types of particular justice then is because they are possible only for people who find themselves in particular situations. Beversluis' claim that particular justice is a species of universal justice is mistaken.

It may help to point out, with regard to the forms of particular justice, that a distinction can be drawn between *practicing justice* and *promoting justice*. The various kinds of particular justice can be *practiced* only by people who occupy certain

---

7. Beversluis, op. cit. Incidentally, Beversluis errs in equating distributive and economic justice. Many instances of distributive justice such as the distribution of grades in a philosophy class have nothing to do with economics.

positions or fill certain roles. But all of us can do things that will *promote* the various kinds of particular justice. For example, we can promote remedial justice by working for the election of honest and competent judges.

Discussions of the Bible's teaching about justice eventually turn to a consideration of the relationship between justice and love. It should be obvious that in some senses, love and justice are closely related. But serious questions about the relationship of love and justice can arise in cases when justice is viewed as a necessary trait of governmental action; for example, criminal justice or governmental control over the distribution of some good or burden. It often seems in such cases that evangelical liberals are prone to a confusion of justice and love. By its very nature, the state is an institution of coercion. It must operate through the use of force. Furthermore, if the state is to appear just, it must operate impersonally. Not to act impersonally would be to discriminate among persons. To the extent that governmental regulation and action is relevant to the particular senses of justice, that justice can only be effected through a state which uses force that is dispensed impersonally in accordance with law. But this analysis of justice conflicts with the nature of love.

Love, by definition, must be given voluntarily; no one can be forced to love whereas the state always must resort to coercion. Moreover, love is always personal in the sense that it is directed at specific individuals. Such discrimination on the part of the state would be a paradigm of injustice. And finally, love should be willing to sacrifice, to go beyond the ordinary moral and legal requirements of a situation. A necessarily coercive state cannot serve as an instrument of love. The state's required use of force is incompatible with the nature and demands of love. As soon as the coercive state enters the picture, love must leave.

When the Christian statist confuses love with justice, he is doing more than simply urging others in his society to manifest a compassionate love for the needy. He is in effect demanding that the state get out its weapons and force people to fulfill the demands of love. This would not be the first time that Christians have made the mistake of encouraging the state to use its vast powers of coercion to help attain their ends. The specter of the Inquisition is clearly visible in the background. No Christian should favor compulsion in bringing people to theological commitment. But is voluntarism any less essential to social virtue? The political liberal's statist approach ignores *giving* and places all its emphasis on *receiving*, on who gets what. And of course, given the nature of statism, *giving* is supplanted by *taking*, a taking effected by the state through its powers of taxation.

Almost every Christian liberal or socialist who writes about social justice refers sooner or later, explicitly or implicitly, to the Old Testament notion of the Year of Jubilee in Leviticus 25:

> Count off seven sabbaths of years—seven times seven years—so that the seven sabbaths of years amount to a period of forty-nine years. Then have the trumpet sounded everywhere on the tenth day of the seventh month; on the Day of Atonement sound the trumpet throughout your land. Consecrate the fiftieth year and proclaim liberty throughout the land to all its inhabitants. It shall be a jubilee for you; each one of you is to return to his family property and each to his own clan. The fiftieth year shall be a jubilee for you; do not sow and do not reap what grows of itself or harvest the untended vines. For it is a jubilee and is to be holy for you; eat only what is taken directly from the fields. (Lev. 25:8-12, NIV).

Stephen Charles Mott sees the Jubilee Year as a divine endorsement of egalitarianism.[8] The fact that, under certain conditions, land would revert to the family of the original owners every fifty years could appear to support the kind of egalitarian redistribution favored by many liberals. Before that conclusion is asserted dogmatically, the entire chapter should be carefully studied in the light of accepted hermeneutical procedures. For example, care should be exercised to distinguish between the

8. *Biblical Ethics and Social Change* (New York: Oxford University Press, 1982) chapter four.

interpretation of the text and its possible applications to cultural settings that differ in important respects. Moreover, the *entire* chapter should be studied; one should not simply extract from the passage those verses that appear to support an egalitarian redistribution of holdings and ignore other verses that suggest something quite different. And finally, serious attention should be given to such questions as these: did Israel ever institute the Jubilee Year? If not, why not? How relevant are principles originally given to a largely agrarian people to the totally different economic and cultural situations of contemporary nations?

A careful examination of Leviticus 25 suggests that many liberation theologians and Christian liberals who appeal to the passage give the chapter a highly selective reading. For one thing, the intended redistribution every fifty years did not affect every form of wealth. The only forms of wealth that were affected were slaves[9] and land outside walled cities. It is important to note that some land was unaffected by the principles of the Jubilee Year. Sold property within walled cities could be redeemed within a year. After the passage of a year, the exchange was regarded as permanent and immune to the changes otherwise affected by the Jubilee (Lev. 25:29-30). Other forms of income such as fishing boats were also excluded from the Jubilee practice. While it may be true that land was the most prevalent and important basis of wealth in ancient Israel, the fact that several forms of wealth were excluded from redistribution in the Jubilee is a fact usually slighted in the writings of liberation theologians.

It is also true that the Jubilee did not benefit all the poor. For example, it did not help immigrants who had no original inheritance. Moreover, given the relatively short life span of people in those days, the fifty year interval between Jubilees made it inevitable that many people (those born after one Jubilee who died before the next) were never helped at all. Many

9. Israelites who had been sold into slavery would be freed in the Jubilee. Slaves who were not Israelites would not be freed.

who are enthusiastic about the Jubilee concept also forget an important fact about a vital effect the Jubilee would have had on such economic activity as the buying and selling of land. Had the Jubilee ever been observed, it would have terminated the buying and selling of land as we know it in favor of leases made more or less valuable by the number of years remaining until the next Jubilee. Under such conditions, anyone contemplating the acquisition of land would know that he was only buying the use of the land for a certain number of years. Thus land would be most valuable in the first years immediately following a Jubilee and worth relatively little in the years just before a Jubilee.

It does seem as though many liberal claims about the Jubilee are exaggerated. If its purpose was to encourage and endorse an egalitarian redistribution of wealth, why were some important forms of wealth unaffected? Why were some of the poor not included? And why was the distribution scheduled at such distant intervals to leave many people who were born and died between Jubilees unhelped? Is it important that the Jubilee could not have been instituted outside Palestine?[10] Is it important that, for all that anyone knows, the Jubilee was never instituted within Palestine? Is it relevant that the principles of the Jubilee could not possibly be instituted today, even within Palestine?

One of the more surprising things about the current interest in finding biblical passages that support a collectivist ideology is this: while people exhibit great ingenuity in discovering hitherto unrecognized implications in ambiguous Old Testament passages, hardly anyone bothers to look at several clear texts in the New Testament. Consider just one:

> Now we command you, brethren, in the name of our Lord Jesus Christ, that you keep away from any brother who is living in idleness and not in accord with the tradition that you received from us. For you yourselves know how you ought to imitate us;

10. This is the case because of the original allotment of the land to the tribes of Israel.

we were not idle when we were with you, we did not eat any one's bread without paying, but with toil and labor, we worked night and day, that we might not burden any of you. . . . For even when we were with you, we gave you this command: if any one will not work, let him not eat. For we hear that some of you are living in idleness, mere busybodies, not doing any work. Now such persons we command and exhort in the Lord Jesus Christ to do their work in quietness and to earn their own living.[11]

One final comment will conclude this chapter. Some Christian social liberals attempt to use the doctrine of Christian stewardship in the service of their ideology. No believer should deny that God is the ultimate owner of all we possess; we are simply stewards or trustees of what He has blessed us with. But some Christian liberals would twist the doctrine of stewardship into the view that the believer must surrender his will and judgment in regard to his holdings to God's surrogate on earth, the state. Once again, the liberal seems incapable of discovering any alternative means to his otherwise worthy ends than giving the state more power and control over the lives of its citizens.

Liberal attempts to ground a statist approach to justice on the Bible leave much to be desired. Such efforts often exhibit questionable hermeneutical principles and they are often inattentive to the classical distinction between a universal and particular sense of justice. Because of the nature of universal justice, it is a simple matter to find justice conjoined in Scripture with love, charity, kindness to the poor, and help for the hungry. But it is irresponsible to infer from these statements that God endorses any contemporary theory of distributive justice.

---

11. II Thess. 3:6ff; see also I Thess. 4:10-11 and Eph. 4:28.

Chapter Seven

The Nature of Capitalism

A prominent feature of much that presently passes for social theology is a negative attitude toward capitalism that ranges anywhere from distrust to absolute contempt. Much of this disdain for capitalism is based on misunderstanding or misrepresentation. That is, many of the complaints about economic malpractice in the contemporary world that are directed against capitalism should in fact be targeted at a competing economic system, *interventionism.*

Capitalism must be distinguished not only from socialism but also from a system with which it is often confused, namely interventionism. Socialism and interventionism are statist systems while capitalism, properly understood, is not.[1] The discussion of capitalism in this chapter has two primary objectives: the elimination of several widespread misconceptions about capitalism and the provision of a model of a free economy that can be contrasted with the socialist and interventionist models.

The first obstacle that any attempt to provide a fair discussion of capitalism must overcome is the problem of terminology. For one thing, the very name most often given to the free market system ("capitalism") was actually coined by Marx as a term of reproach.

1. Many writers think a non-statist socialism is not only a realistic possibility but the only hope of mankind. This utopian brand of socialism will be discussed in a later chapter.

As coined and circulated by Marxism, the term has retained up to the present so much of its hate-filled significance and class-struggle overtones that its usefulness for the purposes of scientific discussion has become extremely questionable. In addition, it provides us with only a very vague notion of the real essence of our economic system. Instead of promoting understanding, it merely arouses the emotions and obscures the truth.[2]

Though use of some other term or phrase, free of the negative emotive connotations of "capitalism," might well contribute to a more enlightened discussion of the issues, no better term seems available. Apparently the most anyone can do is purify its usage.

The term "capitalism" presents problems because it is used in two distinct ways. Sometimes the word is used in an abstract sense to refer to an ideal market economy in which people exchange goods and services in an environment free from coercion, fraud, monopoly, and statist interference with the exchange process. It is important to note, as Von Mises writes, that "The market is not a place, a thing, or a collective entity. The market is a process, actuated by the interplay of the actions of the various individuals cooperating under the division of labor. . . . The forces determining the-continually-changing-state of the market are the value judgments of these individuals and their actions as directed by these value judgments."[3]

"Capitalism" is also used to describe several systems of exchange in the real world that approximate more or less the freedom of the ideal market. These systems differ, of course, in several significant respects from the abstract perfection of the ideal market. The relationship between the ideal market and real economic exchanges is analogous to that between physiology and pathology. No physician ever expects to find every organ in every body functioning perfectly. His study of

2. Wilhelm Ropke, *Economics of the Free Society* (Chicago: Henry Regnery Co., 1960) p. 259.
3. Ludwig Von Mises, *Human Action* (New Haven, Conn.: Yale University Press, 1949) pp.257-258.

physiology provides him with a standard by which he can diagnose pathology. Likewise, the ideal market economy provides standards that can be used to judge the health of economic practices in the real world. Critics of capitalism frequently use the imperfections of existing systems to attack the model. This makes about as much sense as a doctor discarding all his physiology texts because he has never seen a perfectly healthy body.

Deviations from the market ideal occur for several reasons. Frequently, they arise because of statist interference with the market process. Aberrations also occur because of defects in human nature. Human beings naturally crave security and guaranteed success, values not found readily in a free market. Genuine competition always carries with it the possibility of failure and loss. Consequently, the understandable human preference for security leads men to avoid competition whenever possible, encourages them to operate outside of the market, and induces them to subvert the market process through behavior that is often questionable and dishonest. Monopoly is one manifestation of this human propensity to escape the uncertainty and insecurity of the market through the attainment of unfair advantage and special favor.

The Marxist claim that the market leads inevitably to monopoly is false. By definition, the market cannot coexist with monopoly. It is impossible for the market to generate monopolies. Monopolies result from two other causes: (1) the human propensity to escape the uncertainty of the market; and (2) the existence of the only organization powerful enough to permit monopolies to exist, namely, the state. Historically, it is impossible to point to any single monopoly that did not arise as a result of special favors from government.[4] The way to

4. For more on the state's indispensable role in monopoly, see Yale Brozen, "Is Government the Source of Monopoly?", *The Intercollegiate Review*, Vol. 5, Winter 1968-69, pp. 67-68; and Milton Friedman, *Capitalism and Freedom* (Chicago: University of Chicago Press, 1962) chapter VIII. Sometimes conditions in a particular region will give rise to local monopolies. But if force and fraud are excluded and the situation is lucrative enough, others will quickly seek entry to the market.

terminate monopolies is for the state to end its practice of dispensing privileged treatment.

Assessments of capitalism differ widely, of course. Many of the more important objections to the system will be noted in later chapters. The remarks of John Hospers, professor of philosophy at the University of Southern California, are typical of those who support the market system.

> Of all the institutions created in America, the one that has contributed most to the well-being of its inhabitants, more even than any of its institutions of government, is the free-enterprise system. Its beneficiaries are largely ignorant of it; many people, who are its beneficiaries, rail against it; yet it has provided more people with a high standard of living, by far, than any other system ever devised by man. The most ordinary things, which even the poorest people in America take for granted, were either non-existent or extreme luxuries in pre-industrial times. Because of free enterprise, and the technology which it develops, many times more people can live on the face of the earth than had ever been dreamed possible before.[5]

"Capital" is a word used to refer to any resource employed to produce other goods. Resources that can be used as capital include land, labor, and tools (which include complex arrangements of tools such as factories). An additional resource not always recognized as capital is entrepreneurial competence, the ability to bring together other resources in ways that result in a product and make a profit. Advocates of capitalism believe that the limited resources that can be used to produce goods should be privately owned. They believe further that those who have the right of ownership in capital should have the right to transfer ownership. They also believe in freedom of enterprise; that is that any individual or collection of individuals engaged in business should be free to obtain limited resources in a market and be free to sell the products that result from their use of

5. John Hospers, "Free Enterprise as the Embodiment of Justice," in *Ethics, Free Enterprise and Public Policy*, edited by Richard T. DeGeorge and Joseph A. Picheler (New York: Oxford University Press, 1978) p. 71.

the resources. They believe the state should not enter the market to set wages and prices. The process of the market is enough to insure sufficient competition.[6] Entry to the market by new sellers is effectively restrained only when governmental action such as regulation or licensure gives earlier entrants a monopolistic advantage.[7]

There are two basic means by which something can be exchanged. The first is the peaceful, voluntary kind of exchange found in the market. Basically, the peaceful or market kind of exchange can be summed up in the phrase, "If you do something good for me, I'll do something good for you." This is really what market exchange is all about. The reason people exchange in a real market is because they believe the exchange is good for them. They have an opportunity to obtain something they want more for something they desire less.

But there is another way in which exchange takes place, namely, by force and violence. In this violent method of exchange, the basic rule of thumb becomes: "Unless you do something good for me, I'll do something bad to you." Thieves and robbers use this second means of exchange. So does the state as it coerces people into paying its bills through taxation. This second means is the way of threat, force and violence.

One of the most important roles of the market is its function as an instrument for gathering and transmitting information. Each participant in the market process can receive signs or indicators of what desires other people want satisfied at a particular time and for a particular price. Without these indicators, the agent in the market would never know which desires of other people he should aim to satisfy. The prices at which goods and services are selling is one such indicator which supplies important information telling each person in the market how best to direct his own efforts. The key to market

6. It is a serious error to think that the market ideal requires "perfect" competition, whatever this might mean. The competition we are describing only requires *access* to the market.

7. See Friedman, *Capitalism and Freedom*, op. cit., chapter IX.

exchange at any given moment is price. When people's wants are matched by a price they are willing and able to pay, they will buy. When a seller can make a profit (or avoid a greater loss) at this price, he will sell. Without the market mechanism, there would be no way to know the wants and desires of more than a few people. The success of some in the market provides additional indicators that point to directions others should take if they desire similar success. That is, they should provide some service or product at a given price. Of course, when that part of the market becomes too crowded, the signals will change and the wise agent will be ready to switch his activity in accordance with the new signals. The market offers special rewards to those entrepreneurs who are wise or lucky enough to tap new markets.

The informational function of the market is negated, however, by governmental intervention. Factors such as prices and interest rates which might tell people something in an unhampered market become, following the manipulations of the interventionist, distorted and misleading signals that provide no clear message. Governmental intervention that effectively nullified the signals from this mechanical process contributed to many economic crises in America's history. Statist attempts to circumvent the market process and control an entire economic system from some central agency have been notorious failures.

The role of the state should be the same with respect to both economic and political freedom. The rule of law is a necessary condition for both kinds of liberty. The market requires a framework of laws which inform agents in the market which actions are legal. People require protection of their rights in the market, a protection that requires the existence of a minimal state that observes the rule of law. Obviously, the view we are proposing is not a theory of *laissez faire*. According to Hayek, support for the free market does "not mean that government should never concern itself with any economic matters."[8]

8. Hayek, *Constitution*, op. cit., p. 220.

Governmental actions that are inconsistent with the rule of law must, of course, be denounced and corrected. Governmental actions consistent with the rule of law must be evaluated in terms of their expediency. Those that are inexpedient, counterproductive, or harmful should be avoided.

Capitalism is anti-statist because it rejects the statist intervention that subjects the market process to tampering, that negates the market's vital informational function and that results in social costs that far outweigh the presumed advantages. Inflation, which is always the result of the state increasing the money supply, is one social evil that results from such tinkering. As Henry Hazlitt observes, there is an obvious difference

> ... between a general undiscriminatory system of laws against force and fraud, on the one hand, and specific interventions in the market economy on the other. Some of these specific interventions may indeed "remedy" this or that specific "evil" in the short run, but they can do so only at the cost of producing more and worse evils in the long run.[9]

The statist interventions inherent in socialism and the mixed economy are interventions of the second type.

Entirely too much emphasis has been placed on the role that private ownership is supposed to play within capitalism. Obviously, one cannot have capitalism without private ownership. But that is only one small part of the story. For the rest of the story, the essence of capitalism can be summed up in what might be called "the four R's of capitalism": rights, rules, risks and rewards.

(1) A market economy begins by assuming a system of human *rights*, such as the right to make decisions, the right to be free, the right to hold property and the right to exchange what one owns for something else, if that is desired.

(2) But capitalism also includes the right to take *risks*. One

9. Henry Hazlitt, *The Foundations of Morality* (New York: Van Nostrand, 1964) p. 326.

reason societies move forward is because a few people are willing to take risks with their time, money and sometimes their lives. Other people prefer to play it safe and not take such risks. That is their privilege in a free market system. It is interesting to note, however, how often some of those who are unwilling to take risks feel entitled to rewards from those who gambled and won. Many of these non-risk takers never feel obligated to help out by sharing the losses of those who took some risk and lost. Ownership of capital is normally a result of risk-taking coupled with entrepreneurial ability. Such ability involves recognition of a hitherto unrecognized opportunity. Obviously, many people who thought they saw such an opportunity were mistaken. They took their chance and lost. Successful entrepreneurs are those who win more often than they lose. But it is a matter of record that most of the people who believe they have spotted an opportunity end up being wrong. Marxists never talk about the vast numbers of people who lose in a market system.

(3) Capitalism is also impossible without *rules*. The market requires a framework of laws which inform agents in the market which actions are legal. People require protection of their rights in the market, which is also impossible apart from a system of law.

(4) Finally, the market has a place for *reward*. Unless people believe they have something to gain, they will not take risks. Results work two ways; sometimes people win and often they lose. Socialists think it is unjust that a few people end up owning land or businesses. But as long as those people or their forebears acquired their holdings honestly, through their risks and ability and effort, condemnation of their good fortune is unjustified, regardless of how much envy we may feel. If someone thinks he sees an opportunity and is willing to take the accompanying risks, he has a right to a return from his investment. What the socialist wants to do is take from the few risk-takers who got lucky and won and give it to those unwilling or unable to take the risk. Socialists never talk about sharing the losses.

Economic freedom is a necessary condition for personal and political liberty. No one can be free in the political sense if he lacks economic freedom. Economic freedom aids the existence and growth of political liberty by helping to check the concentration of too much power in the hands of too few people. As long as a large percentage of the people in a society exercise ownership control, power within that society will be more widely diffused. No one can be free when he is dependent upon others for the basic economic needs of life. If someone commands what a person can or cannot buy and sell, then a significant part of that individual's freedom has been abridged. Human beings who are dependent upon any one power for the basic essentials of life are not free. When that master becomes the state, obedience becomes a prerequisite to employment and to life itself.

Chapter Eight

Socialism

Like many of the other key terms encountered in this study, "socialism" is not an univocal word. It is a name given to a complex variety of ideologies united in their common opposition to something they call "capitalism." The correctness of socialist perceptions of capitalism varies widely, but rarely approximates reality. Whatever capitalism is, socialists regard it as immoral, irrational, and exploitative. In their view, while capitalism stresses the pursuit of profit, it de-emphasizes basic human values by pandering to greed, materialism, and selfishness. Capitalism is supposed to be unchristian because it is supposedly a system that gives a prominent place to greed and other unchristian values. On the other hand, socialism is thought to encourage basic Christian values such as community.

The various forms of socialism differ, in one sense, in the degree of centralized control they seek to impose on a nation's life and economy. In the case of the state socialisms of Russia, China, Cuba, East Germany, and Bulgaria, the centralized control could hardly be more total and more ruthless. Such state socialisms are a frequent source of embarassment to many professed socialist anarchists in the West who support non-statist forms of socialism. Socialist anarchists never provide any models of how their ideal society will attain order without reinstituting the coercion of the state. Tibor Machan has challenged the realism of non-statist forms of socialism by pointing out that

Leftist and Marxist-oriented anarchists advocate that all property can be held communally or collectively but that no government should exist to keep people from running away with some of it! Anarchocommunism is, at best, a vision; it depends on the idea or faith that humanity will someday develop into a *different species*, one whose members will do everything "right," automatically, in an environment of full abundance, with no scarcity. If that were possible then, indeed, the purpose of government and law could no longer make sense—there would certainly be no need to protect and preserve human rights and legal justice; it would happen anyway, automatically.[1]

Machan's suspicions about anarcho-socialism are justified. While anarcho-socialism presents itself as a workable society for human beings, it is in fact a societal blueprint fit only for an entirely different species, free from all human weaknesses. Machan is correct in rejecting Marxist anarchism as utopian:

It is utopian in the sense that what it promises for some type of creatures is not something that can be held out to human beings with any expectation that the promise might be fulfilled. At any rate, there is no rational reason to anticipate the realization of Marxist communism while there are human beings who ought to find the best form of community life for themselves.[2]

Machan's criticisms of anarchistic socialism have relevance to liberation theology since, following whatever violence may be required to put an end to "capitalism" and bring "socialism" into existence, most liberation theologians look forward to a socialism without the state, a socialism that will be possible because human nature will be drastically renewed. The feasibility of non-statist forms of socialism seems unlikely except in a few small isolated places where the commune is sheltered with state-supported protection and market-produced goods. Between the ominous and unavoidable presence of totalitarian socialist states on the one hand and the illusions of non-statist socialists on the other, there exists a wide variety

1. Tibor Machan, *Human Rights and Human Liberties* (Chicago: Nelson Hall, 1975) p. 143.

2. Ibid., p. 144.

of economic systems that claim to be socialist but which are best viewed as types of *economic interventionism.*

A competent evaluation of socialism is difficult because of its chameleon-like nature. Whenever a particularly embarass-ing problem is noted, socialists demur that *that* is not what they mean by socialism. After the non-market forms of socialism that prevailed sixty years ago were shown to be untenable, socialists altered the nature of their system to make it compatible with some kind of market process, a change that is often ignored in histories of the socialist movement. When contemporary cynics point accusingly at the elitism and imperialism of Soviet socialism, many Western socialists protest that *their* system is different. In the words of one contemporary socialist, the state socialisms found in Eastern Europe and the Soviet Union are to true socialism what "the monsters of the paleolithic era are to present animal species: clumsy, abortive, prototypes."[3] As the socialist Michael Lerner advises, "We do not believe that socialism now exists in any country in the world."[4]

During the first two decades of the twentieth century, the term "socialism" meant *non-market socialism,* an economic system incompatible with any process that would allow the factors of production to be determined by a market. Socialist theorists in those years clearly regarded socialism and any market process as mutually exclusive.

> These were the days when authoritative socialist theoreticians dreamed of the *Naturalwirstschaft,* a society without markets or money, where the planners would run the whole of the industry as though it were Crusoe's island, using only technological calculations "in kind."[5]

3. Serge Mallet, "Bureaucracy and Technology in the Socialist Countries," *Socialist Revolution* 1, No. d (May/June 1970) p. 45.

4. Michael Lerner, *The New Socialist Revolution: An Introduction to its Theory and Strategy* (New York: Delacorte Press, 1973) cited in *The Capitalist System,* edited by Richard C. Edwards, Michael Reich and Thomas E. Weiskopf (Englewood Cliffs, New Jersey: Prentice-Hall, 2nd edition, 1978) p. 532.

5. David Ramsey Steele, "Lange's Theory of Socialism After Forty Years," *Austrian Economics Newsletter,* 1978, Vol. 1, 3, p. 4. Steele documents the non-market nature of socialist theories during the first two decades of the twentieth century.

Socialists predicted that their non-market system would far sur-
pass the productivity of a market system and, in the bargain,
make superior living standards possible for far more people.

About 1920, Ludwig Von Mises advanced the argument that
socialism is not only undesirable but also impossible, because
it makes economic calculation impossible. According to Mises,
production could never be attuned to human wants without
markets to set prices. The impossibility of precise measures of
cost accounting under socialism would result in general
impoverishment. Mises' argument involved three major steps.

First, Mises argued that *economic calculation is necessary
for economic activity*. Without economic calculation, there can
be no economic activity such as buying and selling. Before
people buy and sell, they must calculate whether it is in their
interest to complete the contemplated transactions. A person
might desire both x and y, but be unable to afford both. How
could a rational decision be made without some idea of the com-
parative costs of the two items?

Secondly, *pricing is necessary for economic calculation*. Decisions about whether to buy or not require some indication of
the costs. Without an accurate barometer of how a person will
end up after the exchange, one could not make a rational decision. The basic indicator that signals when people should or
should not engage in economic activity is price.

Thirdly, Mises maintained that *the market is a necessary
condition for pricing*. In theory, some central planning agency
functioning in a totally controlled economy without a market
could place a price on any item. The problem is not just pricing
items, but finding the *right* price, that is, a price high enough
to cover costs and low enough to induce people to buy. Market
prices result from supply and demand. In the market, a merchant can offer his wares at any price he wants. His problem
is whether or not he will find any buyers at that price. If he
does not and still wishes to sell, he must lower his price. Without
markets, economic activity would become chaotic and result in
drastic inefficiencies and distortions. Von Mises' theoretical

attack found empirical support in the Bolshevik attempt to establish non-market socialism in the Soviet Union between 1918 and 1921, when millions starved as a result of the experiment.[6]

Non-market socialism is seldom touted anymore. History books tend to ignore the early non-market forms of socialism. Mises would seem to deserve some credit, even from the socialists, for compelling them to reckon with the need for market pricing mechanisms. Contemporary socialists either ignore the Misean attack or else play a game of scholarly legerdemain. In this latter case, exaggerated claims are made on behalf of one or two feeble attempts to answer the Misean argument. Such an approach frequently cites the efforts of a socialist economist named Oscar Lange to introduce the equivalent of a market system into socialism. What the so-called market socialisms were supposed to show is how a central planning agency could vary prices by a process of trial and error, the key being the rate at which the factory's inventory would be depleted. Steele comments:

> In fact, Lange's system is neither a market nor central planning. It is best classified as a *simulated market*. . . . Everyone would pretend that there was a market and act as if there were a market, but there would be no market in actuality. Such a proposal might have immediately prompted the thought that if the pretense were to achieve the same results as the real thing, it might have to become the real thing. This notion of a pretend market was obscured by Lange's simultaneous advocacy of the marginal rule. It is only because no one really makes losses that Lange's managers can ignore the pursuit of profits. Discussion of the marginal rule often went on without clearly establishing whether its setting was the real market or a pretend market.[7]

6. See Lancelot Lawton, *Economic History of Soviet Russia* (London, 1922) and Paul Craig Roberts, *Alienation and the Soviet Economy* (Albuquerque: University of New Mexico Press, 1971).

7. Steele, op. cit., p. 12. Steele's entire critique should be read. He carefully unmasks fundamental equivocations in the views Lange set forth over the years that make it difficult to believe that many who cite Lange's works have ever read them. For those who would like to read Lange for themselves, the reference is Oscar Lange and Fred Taylor, *On the Economic Theory of Socialism* (New York: McGraw-Hill, 1938).

For example, the internal operations of a factory cannot be
organized without reference to external markets. How does a
factory decide whether it is cheaper to manufacture half-finished
goods within the factory or perhaps buy them more cheaply
from some other factory? Without a system of markets, there
is no way to know. While socialism seeks to eliminate any basis
for determining profits and loss, such considerations cannot be
abolished without destroying the rational basis for all economic
calculation. The failure of socialist attempts to circumvent the
problem by establishing simulated markets is noted by Henry
Hazlitt.

> A number of socialists think they can duplicate the functions
> and efficiencies of the free market by imitating the free market
> in a socialist system—that is, in a system in which the means
> of production are in the hands of the State. Such a view rests
> on mere confusion of thought. If I am a government commissar
> selling something I don't really own, and you are another com-
> missar buying it with money that really isn't yours, then neither
> of us really cares what the price is. When, as in a socialist or
> communist country, the heads of mines and factories, of stores
> and collective farms, are mere salaried government bureaucrats
> who buy foodstuffs or raw materials from other bureaucrats and
> sell their finished products to still other bureaucrats, the so-called
> prices at which they buy and sell are mere bookkeeping fictions.
> Such bureaucrats are merely playing an artificial game called
> "free market." They cannot make a socialist system work like
> a free-enterprise system merely by imitating the so-called free
> market feature while ignoring private property.[8]

Hazlitt points out that most socialist countries including the
Soviet Union practice this imitation of a free market pricing
system. But, he adds, the only reason the socialist's imitation
market economy works, the only reason socialist economies can
function at all, is

> . . . because its bureaucratic managers closely watch what com-
> modities are selling for on free world markets, and artificially
> price their own in conformity. Whenever they find it difficult or

---

8. Hazlitt, *Foundations*, op. cit., p. 304.

impossible to do this, or neglect to do it, their plans begin to go more seriously wrong. Stalin himself once chided the managers of the Soviet economy because some of their artificially-fixed prices were out of line with those on the free world market.[9]

Von Mises did not deny that rational action might still be possible under socialism in regard to small and insignificant matters. But under a system that ignored the factors of profit and loss, it would be impossible for production to be consciously economical. Rational economic production would be impossible. "All economic change, therefore, would involve operations the value of which could never be predicted beforehand or ascertained after they had taken place. Everything would be a leap in the dark. Socialism is the renunciation of rational economy."[10] Von Mises regarded his argument as unanswerable.

Socialism, therefore, presents us with the picture of a system in which comprehensive central planning is impossible. Without making major concessions to a market process, or without imitating prices on the free market, socialist economies would quickly fall into chaos.

THE SOCIALISM OF HERBERT MARCUSE

Many socialists in the West have been so influenced by the writings and ideas of the late Herbert Marcuse that one frequently sees his theories asserted dogmatically without any argument in their support or any credit to their source. Marcuse was an unsparing critic of all advanced industrial societies,

9. Ibid. For general discussions of attempts to refute Mises, see T. J. B. Hoff, *Economic Calculation in the Socialist Society* (London: Hodge, 1949); Friedrich Hayek, *Individualism and Economic Order* (Chicago: University of Chicago Press, 1948); and Roberts, *Alienation and the Soviet Economy*, op. cit. Also worth consulting is Murray N. Rothbard, "Ludwig Von Mises and Economic Calculation Under Socialism," in *The Economics of Ludwig Von Mises*, ed. Laurence S. Moss (Kansas City: Sheed and Ward, 1976) pp. 67-68.

10. Ludwig Von Mises, *Socialism* (New Haven: Yale University Press, 1951) p. 122.

especially the United States. The details of his critique are of less importance in this context than the question of why the people who live in these corrupt societies don't do something about it. Marcuse's answer was that they couldn't. Karl Marx believed that the workers would carry the revolution. But in Marcuse's view, Marx failed to see how the workers would become part of the establishment. Marcuse believed that the worker in an advanced industrial society like the United States becomes corrupted by the influence of the society until he has the same values as the bourgeoisie.

According to Marcuse, modern technology in societies like America eliminates the dissent and conflict that might arise in less advanced societies, by raising false needs and providing false satisfactions. It enslaves people by deceiving them into thinking that the things it gives them are what they really want—better homes and appliances, faster cars, more leisure and luxury. In effect, Americans are so completely dominated, controlled, preconditioned, indoctrinated, and brainwashed that they cannot even recognize their bondage.[11] Man becomes so obsessed by the gadgets he wants to possess, handle, consume, and renew that he ignores the possibility that his obsession may destroy him.

Marcuse attacked this false mass contentment by claiming that the goods produced by the capitalist system provide false satisfaction. First, the system manipulates people into wanting things and then it seduces them into buying them. And then, through such devices as advertising, it increases these wants until the desire to consume becomes compulsive, irrational, and inhuman. The belief of the average man that he is happy only shows how total his bondage is. The things that make man believe he is happy (the electric can openers, the indoor toilets, the diet colas, the boysenberry-flavored breakfast cereals) are the very chains that bind him. Marcuse knew that the members of a capitalist society were not really happy. It made no

11. The ideas of this paragraph can be traced in Herbert Marcuse, *An Essay On Liberation* (Boston: Beacon Press, 1969) p. 11.

difference that the individual identified with his needs and believed they were his. Marcuse knew that the needs were the false product of a repressive society.

No evangelical has to reject every aspect of Marcuse's diagnosis. Portions of it are easily serviceable in a Christian diagnosis of the spiritual ills of a materialistic society whose every conscious moment is spent in the pursuit and the consumption of things. But the appearance of moments of truth in any system of thought should not blind one to differences that may be far more significant or to the implications of a theory that may be absurd or dangerous.

Marcuse believed that men and women need to free themselves from false needs and false consciousness to true needs and a true consciousness. What was required was a new type of human being who could not be seduced by affluence.[12] Only a new consciousness would break the economic, social and political chains that have turned human history into a chronicle of domination and servitude.

It is not enough, however, for Marcuse to argue that men must free themselves from the oppressive influence of false needs imposed by a repressive society; he should also have explained *how* this could be done. And more importantly, he should have shown, given his analysis of man's hopeless condition in the advanced industrial society, that the attainment of liberation and autonomy is possible. Marcuse may have painted himself into a corner. Marcuse created a serious problem for his own position because he claimed that there was no way for the system to correct itself; it was impossible for those dominated by the system to free themselves from it.

Marcuse's plot is thickened by two additonal ingredients that seem to make liberation impossible. First, Marcuse argued that social change would not take place through democratic means because democracy contributes to the plight of society by lulling people into decisions that are against their best interests.

12. See Marcuse's *Essay on Liberation*, op. cit., pp. xiii-xiv and 24-25. See also his *One Dimensional Man* (Boston: Beacon Press, 1964) chapter one.

Advanced industrial societies like the United States appear tolerant of minority views because they know that those views cannot have any effect. Men are not free when they vote and make political decisions, because, according to Marcuse, all who start out under the domination of a repressive society are preconditioned receptacles; they are incapable of criticizing the society or even of heeding a legitimate criticism.

This led Marcuse to his doctrine of "Repressive Tolerance."[13] Because American society is in such perilous danger, Marcuse came to believe that the suspension of free speech and free assembly was justified. After all, there is no real value to freedom of speech; it only insures the propagation of lies. Truth is carried by revolutionary minorities like Marcuse's disciples. Therefore, tolerance should be withdrawn from all those who disagree with Marcuse and extended only to those who make what he called the Great Refusal. Social change can be brought about not by democratic legality but by extra-democratic rebellion. Marcuse wanted to replace democratically supported elites with an elite of his own choosing. Oddly enough, Marcuse admitted that even if his totalitarian measures were put into practice and his followers succeeded in destroying existing society, he could not be sure what would follow.[14]

The questions raised by Marcuse's theory are obvious: How does Marcuse's elite free *itself* from the conditioning that blinds everyone else? And who will provide deliverance from the repressiveness of Marcuse's elite? Such considerations have led several interpreters of Marcuse to see signs of a neo-Nazi mentality in his position.

While the first difficulty Marcuse saw in achieving liberation was the failure of the democratic process, the second problem was the powerlessness of critical social theory to criticize.[15] The very categories of critical theory were developed within the

13. Described in one of three essays in the book, *A Critique of Pure Tolerance* by Marcuse, R. P. Wolff and Barrington Moore, Jr. (Boston: Beacon Press, 1967).
14. See Marcuse's essay in *Critique*, op. cit., p. 87.
15. See Marcuse's *Essay on Liberation*, op. cit., p. xiv.

structure of the system. Furthermore, those who might give the criticism are preconditioned by the system. And finally, those who might otherwise be influenced by a criticism of their society are so brainwashed that they cannot appreciate the force of or understand the nature of the criticism. Thus, there is no one to give the critique, no one to understand, and no critical theory to describe the needed critique. Things indeed look hopeless. But for whom? Perhaps Marcuse created a greater problem for himself than he did for capitalism.

Just when things looked hopeless, Marcuse began to see signs of the Great Refusal all over the place: the revolutions in Vietnam, Cuba, and China; guerrilla activities in Latin America; strains in the fortress of corporate capitalism; stirrings among ghetto populations; and last, but not least, student uprisings.

But the huge and embarrassing lacuna in Marcuse's argument remains. *How, given the total domination of the repressive society, was this opposition possible?* Since Marcuse was claiming that *all* people living in advanced industrial societies are controlled, manipulated, and brainwashed to the extent that they think they are happy, are unable to see their society's faults, and are unable to appreciate criticisms of their society, it follows that *Marcuse's thesis is self-defeating* in the sense that no one, including himself, could have obtained knowledge of the thesis. And even if we grant that Marcuse's books could have resulted from a miracle, he himself would have rejected this hypothesis with scornful derision. A very ironical situation then exists. Thousands upon thousands of socialists have been influenced by a theory which, according to that theory, should have been impossible for Marcuse to discover and should have been impossible for them to understand.

This brief detour into Marcusian socialism is enlightening for several reasons. While almost all socialists profess that their system will expand human liberty, Marcuse acknowledged the deceit of such claims. Freedom may be part of the utopian dream that lies beyond the revolution and the transformation of society. But the seemingly never-ending road to that dream cannot be traveled without the use of repression. As the former French Marxist, Bernard-Henri Levy says somewhere, "Apply Marxism in any country you want, you will always find a Gulag in the end." According to George Gilder,

> The most important event in the recent history of ideas is the demise of the socialist dream. . . . In the United States socialism chiefly rules in auditoria and parish parlors, among encounter groups of leftist intellectuals retreating from the real world outside, where socialist ideals have withered in the shadows of Stalin and Mao, Sweden and Tanzania, gulag and bureaucracy.[16]

Gilder could have added Poland to this list as well.

We have argued that the socialist alternative to a market economy is self-defeating because socialism makes economic calculation impossible. The only reason socialist economies have not failed more frequently is because of their access to pricing information from markets in non-socialist countries. Surely, it would appear, whatever attraction socialism has for its many disciples, its allure cannot be based on rational grounds.

16. Gilder, *Wealth and Poverty*, op. cit., p. 3.

Chapter Nine

The Mixed Economy

The economic system so frequently criticized in the United States does not happen to be capitalism. This fact is conveniently ignored every time some weakness of the system results in blame being placed on the free market system. Advocates of a mixed economy (also called interventionism) believe that statist intervention in economic matters can successfully achieve desired results while falling short of the total controls necessary under socialism. A mixed economy is supposed to be a workable third alternative to the freedom of the market and the total state control of socialism. The state, interventionists claim, only interferes with the market process when necessary to attain some desirable social goal or to avoid some social evil. The interventionist is convinced that many humanitarian goals are unattainable without resorting to occasional and partial statist controls.

The fundamental weakness of the mixed economy was uncovered by Ludwig Von Mises. According to Mises, no logical third alternative to a free market and socialism is possible; no compromise between a market economy and socialism is practical. Partial government controls *must* inevitably fail, which will result in an already bad situation becoming worse. According to Mises,

> The effect of intervention is the very opposite of what it was meant to achieve. If government is to avoid the undesirable consequences it cannot stop with just market interference. Step by step it must continue until it finally seizes control over production from entrepreneurs and capitalists. . . . Government cannot

be satisfied with a single intervention, but is driven on to nationalize the means of production. This ultimate effect refutes the notion that there is a middle form of organization, the "regulated" economy, between the private property order and the public property order.[1]

Interference with market processes will not only fail to attain the interventionist's goals, it will produce conditions worse than those he sought to alter through his controls. This is not to say that things may not appear better in the short run. But in the long run, the unforeseen consequences will be worse. Several examples will make this clearer.

Imagine a state that decides that the price of eggs is too high. Because the state wants to make it easier for poor people to buy eggs, the bureaucrats decide that the imposition of controls on the price of eggs will benefit the poor. Such statists find it easy to congratulate themselves for their humanitarianism and condemn the greedy entrepreneurs who are too interested in making a profit to care that a basic human need is unmet. Because the government cares, it will now act to alleviate that need.

Suppose that the market price for eggs is a dollar a dozen and that the state decides that the quickest way to make eggs more easily available to the poor is to pass a law making it illegal to retail eggs for more than 75 cents a dozen. As soon as the ceiling price drops below the market price, all kinds of unforeseen consequences will occur. First of all, marginal egg producers will find that they are losing money. In every case where a producer's costs (for chicken feed, electricity, gasoline, etc.) exceed his profit under the newly imposed price-ceiling, the state's interference will result in many of them leaving the market. Rather than continue to lose money, many marginal producers will probably sell their chickens and find something more profitable to do. Perhaps they will even give up farming when they discover they can do just as well on welfare.

1. Ludwig Von Mises, *A Critique of Interventionism*, tr. by Hans Sennholz (New Rochelle, New York: Arlington House, 1977) p. 151.

After the state-imposed price-ceiling forces many marginal farmers out of the egg business, fewer eggs will be available, a result that is precisely the opposite of what the bureaucrats originally intended. The statists believed that their intervention into the market would make eggs more available. But as things have turned out, their action has only made eggs more scarce. At this point, the state has two choices. It might decide to regulate prices all the way down the line. That is, the state might decide that it can retain the price-ceiling on eggs and still keep marginal producers in the market by imposing additional controls on the major costs of the chicken farmer. If the marginal chicken farmer cannot stay in business because of the high cost of grain, the way to solve the problem is to impose new price controls on chicken feed. But this simply pushes the problem back to the level of the grain farmer. If *he* cannot make a profit growing grain, he will turn to something else, which will have the effect of making grain more scarce. It soon becomes obvious that the only way governmental intervention into the market can succeed is if it exercises *total* control. But this, of course, would be socialism and mark an end of any experiment in a mixed economy. What began as an innocent, humane, benevolent (and foolish) governmental attempt to make eggs available to more people has not only failed, but has introduced total state control over an entire industry.

The other choice for the statist (other than continuing with partial controls that repeatedly fail) is to admit the mistake and end the controls. Naturally, the removal of controls will produce a number of problems until the disastrous effects of the intervention are gradually overcome through the ordinary processes of the market. In the case of controls on the price of eggs, a removal of the ceiling price in conjunction with the state-induced shortage will result in a dramatic but temporary rise in the price of eggs. The higher price, for which the state is responsible, will cause hardship among the poor people it was trying to help. But the higher price will also be a signal to new producers that this is now a propitious time to enter the egg business. Eventually, the increased supply will begin to meet the demand and the market price will drop. But all this will take time and during the interval, many more people will be forced to go without eggs than before the state's intervention into the market process.

Mises' argument against interventionism, then, maintains that any statist intervention with the market must proceed in either of two directions. Either the state must return to a free market economy and allow the damages resulting from its intervention to ease gradually; or else the state can keep adding more and more controls until all economic freedom ends. There can be no consistent, successful middle ground between the market and socialism.

But interventionists are a remarkably resourceful group. Whenever they are confronted by the failures of their partial controls, they have a predictable response. The failures of the mixed economy are offered as evidence that previous controls did not go far enough; what is really required is *more* interference with the market, not less. In other words, it is always the market process and never interventionism that receives the blame for failure. Through this remarkable slight of hand, past failures are never regarded as reasons for abandoning interventionism. Rather, the mistakes of the past are used as justification for even more total controls in the future. And so, interventionism moves increasingly closer to the total controls of socialism.

Minimum wage laws are a good example of how interventionist policies are counter productive. Defenders of minimum wage legislation claim that the state must intervene in the market to insure that employees, especially disadvantaged and unskilled workers, get a "fair" wage. What this interference does, however, is only increase unemployment among those workers whose productivity is too low to justify the minimum rate.[2] Once again, statist intervention punishes the very people it was supposed to help.

---

2. See Warren L. Coats, Jr., "The Economics of Discrimination," *Modern Age*, 1974, p. 68.

Perhaps the most serious consequence of modern interventionism has been the recent affliction in Western economies of simultaneous inflation and recession. Murray Rothbard provides the background for this crisis:

> For forty years we have been told, in the textbooks, the economic journals, and the pronouncements of our government's economic advisors, that the government has the tools with which it can easily abolish inflation or recession. We have been told that by juggling fiscal and monetary policy, the government can "fine-tune" the economy, to abolish the business cycle and insure permanent prosperity without inflation.[3]

According to orthodox economic theory, any slowing of the economy can be countered by the state's "stepping on the gas" and increasing the money supply and/or federal spending. When inflation becomes the problem, all the government has to do is apply the brakes. But, Rothbard asks, "What can the government do, what does conventional economic theory tell us, if the economy is suffering a severe inflation *and* depression *at the same time*? How can our self-appointed driver, big government, step on the gas and on the brake at one and the same time?" Rothbard contends that "Conventional economic theory is bankrupt." Interventionist policies have created the current crisis and are impotent to solve it. Any continuation of interventionism will only add to the woes. Interventionist economists and politicians usually profess great puzzlement as to the causes of inflation. This is understandable since their manipulations of the economy are its major cause. Henry Hazlitt identifies the nature and cause of inflation:

> Inflation is an increase in the quantity of money and credit. Its chief consequence is soaring prices. Therefore inflation . . . is caused solely by printing more money. For this the government's monetary policies are entirely responsible. . . . The causes of

3. Murray N. Rothbard, *America's Great Depression* (Kansas City, Kansas: Sheed and Ward, 1975) from the Introduction to the Third Edition, no pagination. See also Lawrence W. Reed. "The Silver Panic," *The Freeman*, June, 1978, pp. 366-377.

inflation are not, as so often said, "multiple and complex," but simply the result of printing too much money. . . . If, without an increase in the stock of money, wage or other costs are forced up, and producers try to pass these costs along by raising their selling prices, most of them will merely sell fewer goods. The result will be reduced output and loss of jobs. Higher costs can only be passed along in higher selling prices when consumers have more money to pay the higher prices.[4]

Additional attempts by the state to control the inflation, short of stopping the governmental printing presses and the expansion of credit, cannot stop the inflation.

Price controls cannot stop or slow down inflation. They always do more harm. Price controls simply squeeze or wipe out profit margins, disrupt production, and lead to bottlenecks and shortages. All government price and wage control, or even "monitoring", is merely an attempt by the politicians to shift the blame for inflation on to producers and sellers instead of their own monetary policies.[5]

Rothbard agrees with Hazlitt in holding "that persistent inflation is brought about by continuing and chronic increases in the supply of money, engineered by the federal government."[6] This has been possible since the beginning of the Federal Reserve System in 1913 placed the supply of money and bank credit entirely in the hands of the federal government. Inflation will never stop until the government ends its practice of debasing the currency through legalized counterfeiting.

Statist arguments that governmental intervention with the economy is absolutely necessary to maintain social stability and to enhance freedom and justice are at best a cruel joke. Any effort to produce a system of property hampered by government controls will inevitably produce a crisis which must lead either to an abandonment of those controls or to a surrender

4. Henry Hazlitt, "Inflation in One Page," *The Freeman*, May, 1978, pp. 276f.
5. Ibid., p. 277. George Reisman provides extensive documentation for these claims in his book, *The Government Against the Economy* (Ottawa, Illinois: Caroline House Publishers, Inc., 1979).
6. Rothbard, *Depression*, op. cit., Introduction to Third Edition.

to the total controls of socialism. While partial controls will always result in the interventionist's goals being frustrated, the imposition of total controls would transform the mixed economy into socialism.

Chapter Ten

Is Capitalism Immoral?

Neither socialism nor interventionism appear justifiable on rational grounds. But perhaps there are objections to a market system so dramatic that alternatives to the market must be pursued in spite of their apparent irrationality. Many of the criticisms of a market economy conclude that capitalism must be abolished or restricted because it is unjust or because it restricts important human freedoms. But defenders of the market counter that capitalism is an important bulwark of human liberty and that the abolishment or curtailment of the economic freedom of the market will have serious consequences for political freedom. Defenders of the market also argue that the alleged injustices of capitalism presuppose a narrow and arbitrary sense of justice (i.e., distributive justice). In effect, the critic of capitalism stacks the deck: first, he defines "justice" so that it is necessarily incompatible with the kinds of procedural justice provided by the market; and then he claims to discover empirically a "truth" (i.e., that capitalism is unjust) that actually follows tautologically from his premise. As Irving Kristol explains,

> It is fashionable these days for social commentators to ask, "Is capitalism compatible with social justice?" I submit that the only appropriate answer is "No." Indeed, this is the only possible answer. The term "social justice" was invented in order not to be compatible with capitalism.
>
> What is the difference between "social justice" and plain, unqualified "justice?" Why can't we ask, "Is capitalism compatible with justice?" We can, and were we to do so, we would then

have to explore the idea of justice that is peculiar to the capitalist system, because capitalism certainly does have an idea of justice. "Social justice," however, was invented and propagated by people who were not much interested in understanding capitalism. These were nineteenth century critics of capitalism—liberals, radicals, socialists—who invented the term in order to insinuate into the argument a quite different conception of the good society from the one proposed by liberal capitalism. As it is used today, the term [social justice] has an irredeemably egalitarian and authoritarian thrust. Since capitalism as a socioeconomic or political system is neither egalitarian nor authoritarian, it is in truth incompatible with "social justice."[1]

As our chapters on justice made clear, it is highly debatable whether attempts to apply the notion of distributive justice to massive, complex, spontaneous situations like an entire society make sense.

Can the market be defended against the many attacks leveled against it? What follows in this chapter and the one that follows is an attempt to identify and evaluate actual *arguments* against the market. What frequently pass as criticisms of the market are not arguments but sermons and slogans unsupported by anything remotely resembling reasons or evidence.

Israel Kirzner comments: "One of the most intriguing paradoxes surrounding modern capitalism is the hate, the fear, and the contempt with which it is commonly regarded. Every ill in contemporary society is invariably blamed on business, on the pursuit of private profit, on the institution of private ownership."[2] Capitalism is blamed for every evil in contemporary society including its greed, materialism and selfishness, the prevalence of fraudulent behavior, the debasement of society's tastes, the pollution of the environment, the alienation and despair within society, and the vast disparities in wealth. Even racism and sexism are treated as effects of

1. Irving Kristol, "A Capitalist Conception of Justice," in *Ethics, Free Enterprise and Public Policy*, op. cit., P. 57.
2. Israel Kirzner, "The Ugly Market: Why Capitalism is Hated, Feared and Despised," *The Freeman*, Dec., 1974, pp. 724-5. Kirzner's article is an excellent summary of several fallacies committed by critics of the market.

capitalism. With such an easily identifiable cause of society's ills, it is little wonder the critic has such an easy solution, the replacement of capitalism by a "just economic system," a euphemism for some type of centrally controlled economy.

Many objections to the market result from a simple but clearly fallacious two-step operation. First, some undesirable feature is noted in a society in which a market economy presumably functions. Then, it is simply asserted that capitalism is the cause of this problem. Logic texts call this the *fallacy of false cause.* Mere coincidence does not prove causal connection. Such critics of capitalism conveniently overlook the fact that many of the undesirable features of capitalist societies also exist under socialism.

The cause of the anti-capitalist is helped to no small degree by his audience's inattention to two important factors which hinder understanding of many social problems. The first of these is the history of the problem, for every particular problem occurs at the end of a long chain of causes and effects. When social critics ignore the history of a problem, it is easy to overlook the degree to which past actions of the state have contributed to the problem. The second factor that is easily disregarded is the extent to which an economic system is precisely that, a *system.* In any genuine system, isolated actions that do not produce effects elsewhere in the order are rare. It it not difficult to observe numerous cases in a capitalist economy that are disturbing and deserving of criticism. No great effort is required to denounce immoral and unfair treatment of human beings. But it frequently requires long hours of study and reflection to reveal how the contemptible effect may have resulted from apparently innocent and well-intended pressures applied elsewhere in the system. It is natural for people's moral outrage in such cases to be expressed in the form of demands for immediate state action to remedy the situation. But the critic of capitalism should be honest enough to acknowledge those times when the injurious situation is the complex result of earlier statist intervention.

In this chapter and the next, fifteen arguments against capitalism will be noted. These will be divided into two major categories; (1) those that find capitalism immoral and (2) those that judge it irrational. This chapter will focus on those arguments that charge capitalism with being immoral.

CAPITALISM AND THE MISERY
OF THE WORKING CLASSES

Capitalism has been called immoral because it supposedly contributed to the widespread misery of the working classes in nineteenth century industrialized nations. Friedrich Hayek describes this objection as the

> . . . one supreme myth which more than any other has served to discredit the economic system. . . . It is the legend of the deterioration of the position of the working classes in consequence of the rise of "capitalism" (or of the "manufacturing" or the "industrial system"). . . . The widespread emotional aversion to "capitalism" is closely connected with this belief that the undeniable growth of wealth which the competitive order has produced was purchased at the price of depressing the standard of life of the weakest elements of society.[3]

Bertrand Russell typified those persuaded that early capitalism grew by feeding upon the misery of the working classes that it exploited. In Russell's words,

> The industrial revolution caused unspeakable misery both in England and in America. I do not think any student of economic history can doubt that the average happiness in England in the early nineteenth century was lower than it had been a hundred years earlier; and this was due almost entirely to scientific technique.[4]

3. F. A. Hayek, editor, *Capitalism and the Historians* (Chicago: University of Chicago Press, 1954) pp. 9-10.
4. Bertrand Russell, *The Impact of Science on Society* (New York: Columbia University Press, 1951) pp. 19-20.

Russell failed to inform his reader what evidence he had for his belief that the life of the poor in the eighteenth century was such a happy lark compared to the utter misery produced by the Industrial Revolution.

In 1954, Friedrich Hayek edited a book, *Capitalism and the Historians*, in which he challenged the accuracy of this collection of charges. He pointed to a tremendous bias on the part of historians that has led many of them to ignore the evidence that contradicts the simplistic thesis that the misery of the nineteenth century poor can be laid squarely at the doorstep of capitalism. The undeniable misery of that century should be seen as a continuation of the wretchedness of previous centuries superimposed on the particular conditions of life in a society that was becoming increasingly industrialized. Instead of the poor starving in dirty hovels in the country, they were starving in dirty city slums.

> Several generations of eighteenth- and nineteenth-century writers, clergymen, and assorted social critics tended to lay the blame for every social woe, real or imagined, at the factory doorstep. Many of the intellectuals during the Industrial Revolution looked about and suddenly noticed that there was poverty. But the poverty had been there all along. Why, then, the passionate distaste for the very system which was gradually improving man's material lot? Possibly capitalism was its own worst enemy in this respect, for in raising the general standard of living it made more conspicuous the poverty that still remained.[5]

Poverty did not begin with the advent of capitalism. It may have become more obvious as more and more of the middle class rose to modest affluence, and the contrast between them and the poor became more apparent. Perhaps the poor were also more noticeable because they flocked to urban areas where work was to be found.

The use of child labor in the early years of the Industrial

---

5. Susan Love Brown, et al., *The Incredible Bread Machine* (San Diego: World Research, Inc., 1974) p. 25.

Revolution is a legitimate target of concern. But, once again, it is proper to ask to what extent more general ills in society contributed to the problem. Everyone would prefer a society in which children are free to play games and pick flowers. Unfortunately, that choice was not readily available in those years.

> For many of these children the factory system meant literally the only chance for survival. Today, we overlook the fact that death from starvation and exposure was a common fate prior to the Industrial Revolution, for the pre-capitalist economy was barely able to support the population. Yes, children were working. Formerly they would have starved. It was only as goods were produced in greater abundance at lower cost that men could support their families without sending their children to work.[6]

Was capitalism to blame for the miserable housing conditions of nineteenth century England? The enemy of the market seldom points out the vital role the British government played in this matter. For example, usury laws restricted housing by making it extremely difficult for builders to borrow the money needed to build new housing. There was also a heavy tax on bricks needed for housing as well as a heavy duty on imported timber that might have been used for such building. There was even a tax on windows that penalized the owners of buildings who sought to make more light and fresh air available. Taxes on bricks and tiles also restrained the construction of drains and sewers.

Were conditions really worse than in earlier centuries? The evidence is certainly inconclusive and hardly warrants the dogmatism of Lord Russell. Was capitalism solely responsible for the wretched lot of the nineteenth century poor? More attention should be given to the complicity of the British government in this matter. The truth is, as Hazlitt notes, that

> Capitalism has enormously raised the level of the masses. It has wiped out whole areas of poverty. It has greatly reduced infant

6. Ibid., pp. 25-26.

mortality, and made it possible to cure disease and prolong life. It has reduced human suffering. Because of capitalism, millions live today who would otherwise have not even been born. If these facts have no ethical relevance, then it is impossible to say in what ethical relevance consists.[7]

This first objection to capitalism can only be advanced by those who carefully sift the evidence to fit their preconceived prejudices.

CAPITALISM AND THE EXPLOITATION OF THE WORKING CLASS

Capitalism is often thought to be immoral because it exploits, cheats and robs its own workers. Probably every adult American has heard this charge some time or other. Possibly many unhappy employees have believed that the claim was true, at least in the case of their employer. No doubt, some of them believed correctly. No one in his right mind would suggest that examples of money-grubbing capitalists cheating their workers cannot be found. But that does not happen to be the question. The problem is whether such exploitation is endemic to the system, whether there is something inherent in the free market system that makes such exploitation necessary and unavoidable. Also relevant is the issue of whether it is possible for the free market to adopt measures that would allow workers to have a greater share of the profits. As we shall see, such policies are available, but frequently disdained by the workers themselves.

The charge that capitalism entails the exploitation of the worker has been advanced in two different forms. In the first, it appears in classic Marxist thought in the guise of the famous labor theory of value. Many Marxists have believed that the profit of the capitalist results from his paying his workers less

---

7. Henry Hazlitt, *Foundations of Morality*, op. cit., p. 325.

than the true value of what their labor produced. The theory has never commanded much respect because of its gross over-simplification of the worker's true situation. The theory, for example, ignores the extent to which machines multiply the value of that which human beings produce. A solitary worker using only his own raw materials and his own tools might have some justification for believing that he deserved the full value of the labor he expended on the product. But even this claim would overlook the contribution made to a product's value by the exchange process. The laborer could not be paid for his product until it is sold or exchanged. If the worker is forced to take time off from his manufacturing activity (we might suppose he is making tables) while he seeks a buyer for the table he has finished, the time he loses will be a cost. That is, if he can make one table a day, or five a week, for which he receives twenty dollars apiece, but must spend two days a week selling his tables, that exchange process has cost him two tables or forty dollars. Some people are better at different tasks than others. If the worker can entrust the selling of his tables to someone who is a better salesman (who can, let us say, sell the five tables in half a day), a division of labor is obviously to the worker's advantage. But it also seems clear that the value of the table (that for which it is exchanged) does not result exclusively from the labor that produced it. The exchange process affects the table's value as well. Therefore, even in the most primitive situations, the labor theory of value is over-simplified because it ignores other factors that affect the value of commodities.

But what about a more complex and realistic situation where a worker, using raw materials purchased and transported to him at someone else's expense and using machines purchased at some risk by an enterprising entrepreneur, is enabled to make ten tables a day? Does his increased productivity entitle him to ten times more pay? Marx's labor theory of value ignores the extent to which machines multiply a worker's productivity. Certainly, someone had to pay for the machines; someone had

to invent them. Someone had to have the initiative t̶
risks involved in investing money for the whole e̶n̶t̶e̶r̶p̶r̶i̶s̶e̶.
What is so immoral about the fact that the person who made
these investments and took these risks receives a return from
the added productivity of the workers who use his capital? It
seems clear that if capitalism is to be condemned for robbing
its workers, it must be on some basis other than the labor theory
of value.

But the claim of worker exploitation might be made in a
different way. Perhaps it can be argued that capitalists exploit
their workers by claiming *excess* profits. That is, even if it is
conceded that the capitalist is entitled to some return on his
risk and investment, there is a line between a fair return and
obscene profits. In most cases (except those in which the
intervention of a state has given some corporation a marked
advantage over its competition), excessively large profits would
be a temporary circumstance. If some company through insight
or luck were fortunate to gain such dominance of a market as
to produce huge profits, this fact would quickly lead other
entrepreneurs to enter the same market. The history of
American business is full of companies that gained an uncom-
monly large share of a market for a time, only to lose it. Many
of those companies no longer exist. Perhaps it is only fair that
the workers in such a company receive a share of these larger
profits. But fairness would also seem to require that they be
willing to share in some of the losses and sacrifices that often
precede and follow the unpredictable periods of prosperity.

Many businessmen would not object to their employees
participating in a profit sharing plan. But it would seem fair
to require that if the employees of a particular company want
a guaranteed share of the profits, they should be willing to share
some of the risks. Robert Nozick has addressed this question.[8]
He notes that whatever the lot of the working class in the past
may have been, many members of the working class today have

---

8. Nozick, op. cit., pp. 253-262.

access to cash reserves. Large cash reserves also exist in union pension funds. According to Nozick, the fact that large segments of the working force in America could invest "raises the question of why this money isn't used to establish worker-controlled factories. Why haven't radicals and social democrats urged this?"[9] If the reply is given that workers themselves "lack the entrepreneurial ability to identify promising opportunities for profitable activity, and to organize firms to respond to these opportunities," then why don't the workers "*hire* entrepreneurs and managers to start a firm for them and then turn the authority functions over to the workers (who are the owners) after one year?"[10] Nozick thinks the reason is obvious.

It's *risky* starting a new firm. One can't identify easily new entrepreneurial talent, and much depends on estimates of future demand and of availability of resources, on unforeseen obstacles, on chance, and so forth. Specialized investment institutions and sources of venture capital develop to run just these risks. Some persons don't want to run these risks of investing or backing new ventures, or starting ventures themselves. Capitalist society allows the separation of the bearing of these risks from other activities. The workers in the Edsel branch of the Ford Motor Company did not bear the risks of the venture. In a socialist society, either one *must* share in the risks of the enterprise one works in, or everybody shares in the risks of the investment decisions of the central investment managers. There is no way to *divest* oneself of these risks or to choose to carry some such risks but not others . . . as one can do in a capitalist society.[11]

Nozick points out how often some people who are unwilling to assume risks "feel entitled to rewards from those who do and win; yet these same people do not feel obligated to help out by sharing the losses of those who bear risks and lose."[12] He asks, "Why do some feel they may stand back to see whose ventures turn out well . . . and then claim a share of the success; though

9. Ibid., p. 255.
10. Ibid.
11. Ibid., pp. 255-256.
12. Ibid., p. 256.

they do not feel they must bear the losses if things turn out poorly, or feel that if they wish to share in the profits or the control of the enterprise, they should invest and run the risks also?"[13] Capitalism affords a significant advantage to those people who would shift the risks to others and prefer the security of a fixed income. They can have the security they want. But they should not begrudge the individual who shouldered the risk any profit he might be fortunate enough to receive from his investment.

In summary, the argument that capitalism is immoral because it necessarily exploits the worker by allowing the capitalist excess profits at the worker's expense is a mixed bag. It is perfectly consistent with a market system to defuse this possibility by offering the workers a chance to share in all "excess profits," whatever this might be taken to mean. But why should workers be given an opportunity to share any winnings without also bearing an equal responsibility to share the risks and possible losses? Thus, it is clearly false that capitalism necessarily involves the exploitation of the worker.

CAPITALISM AND THE EXPLOITATION OF POORER COUNTRIES

The third argument claims that capitalism is immoral because it leads to the exploitation of underdeveloped countries. Something like this is usually meant whenever capitalism is equated with imperalism. Richard T. DeGeorge points out the weakness of this charge.

> Industrial countries today still import raw materials from other countries which are sometimes less developed. This fact by itself does not equal exploitation. Moreover, the raw materials can be sold to countries run more or less on the capitalistic model or to countries run on the socialistic model. The price at which the material is sold does not depend on the economic system of the

13. Ibid.

buyer country. Hence, the case cannot be sustained that the capitalistic countries depend on exploitation unless the socialistic countries are to be blamed likewise. The evil, in that case, would not be an evil of capitalism, but an evil of well-to-do or industrial as opposed to poor and non-industrial countries.[14]

Countries that take advantage of weaker nations are those that are richer, more powerful or more industrialized. But these advantages are exercised by socialist nations as well as nations that approximate a market economy. The claim that capitalism necessarily involves the exploitation of weaker and poorer nations can only be made by those who ignore the equal complicity of socialist states. The argument is another example of the Fallacy of False Cause. It presumes that because nation A exploited nation B, and because A approximated a free economy, it was nation A's capitalism that caused the exploitation. This reasoning ignores the other features of A (possible militarism, power, wealth, etc.) that are more likely causes, especially since these other features are also found in socialist states that practice exploitation.

CAPITALISM PANDERS TO GREED AND SELFISHNESS

Another reason some reject capitalism as immoral is their belief that it panders to greed and selfishness. According to William Coates, "In a capitalist society the primary virtues are competitiveness, greed and ambition. These virtues, it is said, provide the necessary energy which motivates the whole system."[15] The claim that the market panders to human greed is false. A proper understanding of the operation of the market will show how the market, in fact, neutralizes greed. One may lust after the property of another all he wants. But as long as

14. Richard T. DeGeorge," Moral Issues in Business," in *Ethics, Free Enterprise and Public Policy,* op. cit., p. 11.
15. William Coates, *God in Public* (Grand Rapids: Eerdmans Publishing Co., 1974) p. 184.

the rights of the second party are protected, the greed of the first individual cannot harm him. As long as the first person is prohibited from using force, theft or fraud, his greed for another's property must be channeled into the discovery of products or services for which people are willing to exchange their own holdings. Greed can never harm another person so long as his rights are protected. If Mr. X is going to satisfy his greed within a market system of rights, he is going to have to offer others something that they want in exchange. His greed must lead him to a product or service which others are willing to barter for. Thus, every person in the market has to be other-directed. Each must ask himself what other people want and how he can best service those wants. Therefore, any greed that might operate in the market involves a paradox. The market is one area of life where concern for the other person is required. The market, then, does not pander to greed. It is rather a mechanism that allows natural human desires to be satisfied in a nonviolent way. The alternative to free exchange is violence.

The market is an instrument that enables people to attain individual goals in a voluntary, nonviolent way. It is difficult to see how the pursuit of individual goals, which the market makes possible, is equivalent to selfishness. It requires a great deal of question-begging to equate even the pursuit of monetary profit with selfishness. Since profit can be a means to other ends, it can be used for selfish or for altruistic purposes. The market only reflects the values of the people who use it. The pursuit of goals, even profits, is not selfish per se. Moreover, the needy members of a society cannot be helped by the productive members until the economic system produces at least enough to go around. The free market makes private and public charity possible in this way. No competitive economic system can match the market's record of productivity.

WINNERS AND LOSERS IN THE CAPITALIST SYSTEM

Capitalism is accused of being immoral because it inevitably produces situations in which some people gain at the expense of others. Objections like this assume that capitalism is exploitative in the sense that the seller always takes unfair advantage of the buyer, that he *uses* the buyer, in some sense. The assumption is that some competitive economic system, socialism presumably, would create a climate in which buyers and sellers would become much more considerate of each other. This charge is clearly based on a false analogy. When two people play checkers, it is true that only one of them can win; the other must lose. But it is a mistake to assume that because the entrepreneur has made a profit, he has won and the buyer has lost. On the contrary, the market is one place where one person's gain need *not* be another's loss. The market is one place where both parties can win. It is just as true that the seller *uses* the buyer. In the market, exchanges occur when both parties get something they wanted. Unless both parties to an exchange were satisfied, they would not have bothered. Whether the exchange really was mutually beneficial is beside the point; it took place because both sides *believed* it was beneficial. As long as force and fraud are excluded from economic exchange, both parties can walk away as winners.

This analysis is pertinent to employer-employee relationships. Some people assume that the employer always wins at the expense of his employees. But in this form of market exchange, the employee is trading his time, effort, and labor for something else he wants more, his salary. Since he is getting something he wants, he is anything but a victim. This argument does not assume for one moment that all or even many such exchanges are idyllic. But the point is that there is nothing inherently exploitative in the exchange process. Now, of course, exchanges occasionally take place under conditions where someone does in fact lose. Because conditions may be unfavorable, a person may be forced to sell something at a time or for a price he finds inconvenient, while another person who can wait for more opportune circumstances may be able to make a profit. Under the wrong conditions, any buyer or seller might come away from a transaction as the loser. But even in such cases, the agent is moved by the belief that the exchange is preferable to some alternative. Nor does this argument ignore the problem of corruption within any system. Certainly there are dishonest employers; there are also dishonest employees who collect a full day's wages for less than a full day's work. The market is a tool that is used by both moral and immoral people. It hardly seems fair to blame it for the immoral practices of some without also praising it for the indispensable service it affords to moral people.

THE PURITANICAL ARGUMENT

The American economist, John Kenneth Galbraith, has made a fair amount of money writing books in which he argues that capitalism is immoral because it encourages people to spend their money on trivial, useless, or immoral products. This popular objection to capitalism is often, for obvious reasons, dubbed the Puritanical Argument. A free market, it claims, produces too many of the wrong goods. The market floods society with a surplus of trivial, worthless, and perhaps even dangerous items.

> The market for consumer goods is now characterized by the sale of more and more useless items. Those items that are still necessary are more and more laden with useless accessories, fringes, decorations and anything that can be used to increase the price. Thousands of virtually identical products—produced with enormous waste in duplication—compete for consumer's attention in supermarkets and department stores under different brand names. To make the system work, billions are spent on advertising to assure a customer's preference for one identical product over another.[16]

The proponent of the Puritanical Argument often omits an

16. Tom Christoffel, David Finkelhor and Dan Gilbarg, editors, *Up Against The American Myth* (New York: Holt, Rinehart and Winston, 1970) p. 15.

important part of his conclusion. Rothbard fills in the gaps: "If people are immoral enough to choose whiskey rather than milk, cosmetics rather than educational matter, then the State, they say, should step in and correct these choices."[17] The fact that improper choices of individual citizens will have to be corrected by the hopefully more intelligent decisions of bureaucratic elites arouses concern that the cure could be worse than the disease. The argument implies that

> . . . consumers ought to be deprived of freedom of choice, and
> . . . government bureaucrats, full of wisdom . . . should make their consumptive choices for them. The consumers should be supplied, not with what they themselves want, but with what bureaucrats of exquisite taste and culture think is good for them. And the way to do this is to tax away from people all the income they have been foolish enough to earn above that required to meet their bare necessities, and turn it over to the bureaucrats to be spent in ways in which the latter think would really do people the most good . . . all supplied, of course, by government.[18]

But who will appoint the governmental elitists who will make these decisions for the consumer? It would hardly be consistent for the proponent of this argument to maintain that the government should be elected democratically. After all, if the people cannot be trusted to make relatively minor economic decisions in their normal everyday affairs, how can they be trusted in the much more important matter of recognizing those qualified to lead them? If the power of modern advertising is so irresistible that the typical consumer cannot freely choose between brands of breakfast cereal, his susceptibility to persuasion certainly disqualifies him as a competent judge of political leadership. Rothbard has a point when he suggests that "anyone who advocates governmental dictation over one area

17. Murray N. Rothbard, *Power and Market* (Kansas City: Sheed Andrews and McMeel, Inc. 2nd edition, 1977) p. 208.

18. Henry Hazlitt, "Planning vs. the Free Market," *Essays in Liberty* (Irvington-on-Hudson, New York: The Foundation for Economic Education, 1963) Volume X, pp. 183-184.

of individual consumption must logically come to advocate complete totalitarian dictation over all choices."[19]

But aside from its sinister implications for human liberty, how fair is the kind of reasoning found in the Puritanical Argument? Imagine an individual who visits a particular restaurant so frequently and eats so gluttonously that he gains thirty pounds in just a few weeks. Suppose one day that the now badly overweight gentleman begins to berate his regular waiter for his corpulence. Who really is at fault? All the waiter did was bring the meals that the customer ordered. That was his job. The real fault obviously rests with the diner. In a similar way, the advocate of the Puritanical Argument blames the market for the mistakes of the consumers. If an economic system permits the consumer to make free choices, it can hardly be blamed if the consumer chooses unwisely. Surely the consumer has to bear much of the responsibility for trivial or poor quality goods. One might question the ethics of the businessman who produces a poorer quality product for a lower price. But if the consumer is willing to pay the price of lower quality in trade for lower cost, should he not have that privilege? The obvious rebuttal to the Puritanical Argument is that "the market economy is simply a resultant of individual valuations, and thus . . . the fault lies with the valuations, not the economic system."[20]

The claim that all bad habits and bad tastes of consumers are caused by wicked producers is equally suspect.

> The philosophy is not only based on the doctrine depicting the common people as guileless suckers who can easily be taken in by the ruses of a race of crafty hucksters. It implies in addition the nonsensical theorem that the sale of articles which the consumer really needs and would buy if not hypnotized by the wiles of the sellers is unprofitable for business and that on the other hand only the sale of articles which are of little or no use for the

19. Rothbard, *Power*, op. cit., Several aspects of this problem have already been covered in our earlier discussion of Marcuse.
20. Ibid.

buyer or are even downright detrimental to him yields large profits.[21]

The irony of statists who bemoan the consumer's lack of free choice under a market economy and then urge that all economic choices be turned over to a central planning committee should not be overlooked. The inconsistency is so obvious as to appear hypocritical. Even though consumers under a market economy are open to persuasion from a variety of sources including parents, friends, as well as advertisers, they still make choices among a variety of enticements. If this were not true, it would be impossible to account for the existence of so many competing advertisements. The power of consumers to choose freely, and by those choices influence offerings of the market, is far greater under capitalism than under the centralized planning desired by the critics of the market.

The charge of planned obsolescence that usually accompanies the Puritanical Argument is clearly incompatible with the evidence. If manufacturers really did design products that quickly fell apart, foreign competition and consumer resentment would soon drive them out of business. What the enemy of the market sees as planned obsolescence is frequently continued improvement of new products that does indeed produce dissatisfaction with the older and now inferior product. The old Ford Model T was profitable for years at the same time that it avoided planned obsolescence. But Ford was eventually compelled to change its design by the consumer's desire for a new and better product. Competition in the tire industry has produced remarkable advances in the product. Only competition would have worked so successfully in producing this search for improvement. Would a state-owned monopoly unchallenged by any competitor have had much incentive to improve its product? More than likely, a government-run industry would have remained content with the old product.

21. Ludwig Von Mises, "On Equality and Inequality," *Modern Age*, 1961, p. 142.

THE MORALITY OF ADVERTISING

Capitalism is held immoral by many because it depends upon the morally questionable practice of advertising which supposedly creates artificial need, manipulates people, and debases taste. The economist, Israel Kirzner, notes how "Advertising, a pervasive feature of the market economy, is widely misunderstood and often condemned as wasteful, inefficient, inimical to competition, and generally destructive of consumer sovereignty."[22] Complaints about the questionable ethics and bad taste of much contemporary advertising strike a raw nerve with many reflective people. Clearly, what often passes for advertising is less than honorable or uplifting. But on the other hand, it is important to recognize the essential function advertising serves in a free society. It is a vital source of information for the buyer, alerting him to new products or new opportunities. The charge that advertising unfairly passes along an unnecessary cost to the consumer results from a failure to grasp an important fact about production costs. Kirzner explains that it

... might seem that the entrepreneur's function is fulfilled when he transforms an opportunity to produce a potential product into an opportunity for the consumer to buy the finished product. Consumers themselves were not aware of the opportunities this production process represents; it is the superior alertness of the entrepreneur that has enabled him to fulfill his task. It is not sufficient, however, to make the product available; consumers must be aware of its availability. If the opportunity to buy is not perceived by the consumer, it is as if the opportunity to produce has not been perceived by the entrepreneur. It is not enough to grow food consumers do not know how to obtain; consumers must know that the food has in fact been grown! Providing consumers with information is not enough. It is essential that the opportunities available to the consumer attract his attention, whatever the degree of his alertness may be. Not only must the

22. Israel Kirzner, "Equilibrium versus Market Process," in *The Foundations of Austrian Economics*, ed. Edwin G. Dolan (Kansas City: Sheed and Ward, 1976) p. 121.

entrepreneur-producer marshal resources to cater to consumer desires, but also he must insure that the consumer does not miss what has been wrought. For this purpose advertising is clearly an indispensable instrument.[23]

Kirzner is clearly correct when he concludes, "All costs are in the last analysis selling costs."[24]

Advertising also insures accessibility to markets by new and thus relatively unknown sellers. Thanks to advertising, it is easier for new sellers to gain entry to the market.[25] It is untrue that advertising increases the cost of the product, a cost that must be absorbed by the victimized consumer. Advertising usually reduces price.[26] Advertising should be viewed as one sign of the entrepreneur's basic insecurity. Every day, when he opens for business, he lacks sufficient information to tell him what will happen that day. He is at the mercy of an innumerable number of unknown factors. If he's lucky and guesses right, he can make a profit. If he's unlucky or guesses wrong, he will lose. He can never be sure what the market will do to him today. Consequently, the advertiser is trying to allay his fears and draw the consumer's attention to his product or service. While we may not like the form his advertising takes, it is an indispensable part of a free market. The questionable values frequently observed in some types of advertising reflect as much on the standards of the potential customer as on the character of the advertiser. The blame for questionable advertising falls on the advertising agency, the seller *and* the consumer. Harold Demsetz notes ironically that "intellectuals, so dedicated to the principle of free speech that they actively defend pornography, can hardly object to advertising because commercials are done poorly."[27]

23. Ibid., p. 122.
24. Ibid., p. 123.
25. All of these questions about advertising are addressed with competence in the book, *Advertising and Society*, ed Yale Brozen (New York: New York University Press, 1974).
26. See Brozen, op. cit., p. 84.
27. Harold Demsetz, "Advertising in the Affluent Society," in Brozen, op. cit., p. 70.

Philip Nelson summarizes the problem of advertising nicely.

> In summary, while advertising is not exactly a shiny white knight distributing Ajax as it gallops, it is not evil incarnate. On the average, advertising is doing a good job, making an important contribution to the information of consumers and the competitive operation of markets. But advertising is an institution that can be improved. Unfortunately, most of the proposals that have been made to improve upon advertising would make matters worse. Basically, these reforms are flawed by failure to understand how advertising works. As in most economic problems, a "good heart" is insufficient equipment to produce a better world.[28]

Thus, while advertising is indeed an essential part of a free market system, claims that it is a morally questionable or taste-debasing practice are guilty of blaming a legitimate practice because of its misuse by some. The same reasoning would abolish the practice of medicine because some use it corruptly.

CAPITALISM AND PUBLIC GOODS

Some maintain that capitalism is immoral because of its inability to provide basic public goods that are not clearly profitable. John Arthur and William Shaw articulate this charge by arguing that "the market mechanism cannot provide certain goods which are in everyone's interest—a decent urban environment, pollution-free air, public transportation, parks—goods which lack an attractive profit angle."[29] In a similar vein, Norman Bowie and Robert Simon maintain that the

> . . . market mechanism does not apply to certain goods—most of them in the public sector. For private goods, my consumption affects your consumption. You cannot eat the apple that I have eaten. For this reason each of us will express our true desires

28. Philip J. Nelson, "The Economic Value of Advertising," Ibid., p. 64.
29. John Arthur and William H. Shaw, *Justice and Economic Distribution* (Englewood Cliffs, New Jersey: Prentice-Hall, 1978) p. 180.

for the apple in the market place. The price one is willing to pay is a measurement of that desire. Hence, the pricing mechanism rations scarce goods according to one's willingness to pay. Regrettably, this rationing scheme does not work for public goods. You can drive on the same road that I drive on. Hence, when it comes time to fix the road, you will understate the price you are willing to pay, hoping that I will pick up the burden. Of course, as rational egoists we all think this way, and the real value of the road to us is not reflected in the market place as is the real value of the apples.[30]

In other words, capitalism's great efficiency in meeting private needs where profits can be made is not duplicated in cases of public needs that provide little opportunity for profit. In fact, capitalism is notoriously inefficient in such cases.

Clearly, this line of argument applies only to extreme libertarians or anarcho-capitalists who reject entirely any role for the state. But this option has already been eliminated.[31] Most defenders of the market admit the possibility that some public goods may require state action for their implementation. Milton Friedman, for example, acknowledges that we may "want to do through government some things that might conceivably be done through the market but that technical or similar conditions render it difficult to do in that way. These all reduce to cases in which strictly voluntary exchange is either exceedingly costly or practically impossible."[32] This would certainly be true in the case of "general access roads, involving many points of entry and exit [where] the costs of collection would be extremely high if a charge were to be made for the specific services received from each individual . . ."[33]

Defenders of the market like Friedman insist, however, that

30. Norman E. Bowie and Robert L. Simon, *The Individual and the Political Order* (Englewood Cliffs, New Jersey: Prentice-Hall, 1977) p. 195.

31. My objections to anarcho-capitalism can be found in chapter one of my *Freedom, Justice and the State* (Lanham, Maryland: University Press of America, 1980).

32. Milton Friedman, *Capitalism and Freedom*, op. cit., pp. 27-28. Most of Friedman's book is relevant to this problem.

33. Ibid., p. 30.

the scope of such public goods is much smaller than is usually believed. For example, the provision of a quality education probably requires funding through taxation. But as Friedman has shown, it does not require public school systems. The quality of education would be greatly increased if schools actually had to compete for pupils on a free and open market. Friedman suggests that the state return tax money to parents in the form of vouchers which the parents could use to pay for their children's education at any school they choose. The ensuing competition would quickly result in poorer quality schools being driven out of the educational market.[34]

Present federal policies that obscure the true costs of public goods to those who benefit from them are unfair. For example, people who use public transportation in New York City should pay the full costs of that system. Under present policies of the federal government, the losses of the New York system are subsidized by taxpayers in the rest of the country whose federal tax dollars are channeled to the municipal government of New York City. The nature of such hidden costs lessens the incentive of politicians to hold down costs.

This objection to capitalism appears clearly irrelevant because few defenders of the market deny the existence of all public goods. The statist's argument diverts attention away from the more serious ethical implications of continual expansions of the sphere of these allegedly public goods. Present tax policies that disguise the true costs of many such "services" should be abandoned.

THE PROBLEM OF NEIGHBORHOOD EFFECTS

A fairly recent addition to the list of objections against capitalism argues that capitalism is immoral because the pursuit of profit frequently results in serious side effects, the cost of which is unfairly passed along to people who should not have

34. See Friedman, op. cit., chapter VI.

to pay. The environmental crisis has shown that the consumption and production of many goods and services can produce serious side effects. If the things that are presently polluted like air and water were property, no one would be free to use them as garbage dumps. That is not to say these things would cease to be polluted; it is to recognize that people could not pollute them *freely*, that is, without being obliged to pay the costs of pollution. According to David (not Milton) Friedman, "if the pollution were done to something that belonged to someone, the owner would permit it only if the pollutor were willing to pay him more than the damage done. If the pollutors themselves owned the property they were polluting, it would pay them to stop if the damage they did were greater than the cost of avoiding it; few of us want to dump our garbage on our own front lawns."[35]

Short of terminating the entire human race, there is no way to end pollution. Even then, non-human life would continue the process of pollution to some extent. The point to the pollution problem is to insure that the damage done remains less than what it would cost to avoid the pollution. But who should pay for reducing or eliminating the pollutants? Two companies manufacturing the same product might both produce the same amount of air pollution. As long as both accepted the cost of reducing the pollution and passed the cost on to the consumer in the form of a higher price, the problem could be eased. But if only one company treated pollution as an internalized cost, its product would be more expensive than that of the free-loading company which would then gain a distinct market advantage. One way to handle this is to assign property rights to the air that is polluted. This would require any company polluting the air to pay a price high enough to compensate the owner of that property right for the poorer quality of air. However, the problems of converting something like air into property where individual property rights can be easily

35. David Friedman, *The Machinery of Freedom* (New Rochelle: Arlington House, 1978) p. 139.

identified are too obvious to mention. One solution is to admit a limited role to the state and assign these property rights to the government.

> If pollution control is to be handled by government, it should be done by [letting] the government set a price, per cubic foot of each pollutant, for polluting. Such a price might vary according to where the pollution is created; air pollution in Manhattan presumably does more damage than in the Mojave Desert. Every pollutor, from the United States Steel Corporation down to the individual motorist, would have to pay. If the cost of avoiding pollution is really high, the firm will continue to pollute—and pay for it. Otherwise, it will stop. If the voters think there is still too much pollution, they can vote to raise the price; it is a relatively simple issue. . . . If pollutors must pay for their pollution, however avoidable or unavoidable, we will rapidly find out which ones can or cannot stop polluting.[36]

Critics of technology seldom combine their criticism of the products of technology with their own willingness to forsake the advantages of technology. Many take full advantage of their society's technology and then hypocritically denounce the by-products of the technology from which they benefit.

CAPITALISM AND HUMAN ALIENATION

Finally, capitalism is condemned as immoral because it causes human alienation. Karl Marx, utilizing insights borrowed from the philosophy of Hegel, first made this charge in some of his early manuscripts which were written several years before *The Communist Manifesto*.[37] Marx believed that capitalism causes worker alienation in several ways. First, the worker is alienated from that which he produces. Marcuse was simply echoing this view when he claimed that the worker becomes dominated and

---

36. Ibid., pp. 140-141.
37. These manuscripts along with a helpful introduction can be found in *Karl Marx, Early Writings*, translated and edited by T. B. Bottomore (New York: McGraw-Hill Book Co., 1964).

controlled by the things created by the economic system. Secondly, the worker is estranged from the labor process itself. No great effort is required to note how many men and women hate their jobs. This alienation from one's work is not restricted to those who must labor at menial, repetitive, boring, dirty, or degrading occupations. Even professional golfers and philosophers have been known to hold an occasional loathing for their jobs. Thirdly, the worker under capitalism becomes alienated from other men, a fact easily observed by attending to the widespread competitiveness, hostility, and animosity among human beings. And finally, the poor worker even becomes alienated from himself. Surely, writes DeGeorge on behalf of those persuaded by this argument, "There is something wrong with a society that values goods more than people, that dehumanizes people in the labor process, and that fragments human beings into competitors, preventing them from social cooperation and mutual respect."[38]

The evidence does suggest that all of the forms of alienation noted by Marx exist under capitalism. But surely such alienation is not a feature of capitalist societies alone. As DeGeorge indicates,

> . . . in those societies in which the private ownership of the means of production has been done away with, there is no perceptible decline in alienation, in the desire for goods, in the dehumanization that is tolerated in factories, and so on. And in societies which continue to have private ownership of the means of production, we find growing numbers less interested in goods than their parents; we find a stronger defense of human rights than elsewhere; we find a consciousness that certain types of work can be dehumanizing and stultifying and attempts to change such conditions; and we find not only competition but also cooperation and a willingness to work together.[39]

It is difficult to believe that a garbage collector in Moscow is any happier with his job than a garbage collector in Boston.

38. DeGeorge, op. cit., p. 12.
39. Ibid.

Alienation and dehumanization are serious problems, but it is simply not true that they result only from conditions existing in capitalist societies and vanish once societies have become socialist.

The Marxist theme of alienation recurs often in the writings of liberation theologians. We think their use of this theory reveals the one-sidedness of their world view. Human alienation should be addressed but it is no more an exclusive effect of capitalism than baldness. One thing strangely missing from the writings of liberation theologians is a discussion of a fifth variety of human alienation that Karl Marx ignored. The Bible gives prominent attention to the fact that every member of the human race is alienated *from God.* In fact, Scripture clearly implies that all of the forms of human alienation that concern contemporary Marxists result in some way from man's more fundamental alienation from his Creator. Recognition of this biblical truth could introduce an entirely new dimension into discussions of alienation.

CONCLUSION

We have examined ten arguments offered in support of the conclusion that capitalism should be abolished because it is immoral. In every case, we have found, the arguments fall short of their objective. *Capitalism is not inherently immoral.* It is a system that is used both by moral and immoral people. Statist systems, we believe, like socialism and interventionism contain far more potential for evil, given the nature of human beings in this, the real world. Many of the critics of capitalism, we have found, have no idea what they are talking about. Many of the effects they find so appalling are in fact the products of economic interventionism. More attention needs to be given to the positive and moral contribution capitalism has made toward elevating the quality of human life. No Christian need be

ashamed to count himself a defender of capitalism. Whether this
is also true of socialism or interventionism is less clear.

Chapter Eleven

Is Capitalism Irrational?

In addition to the moral arguments against capitalism noted in chapter 11, capitalism is alleged to suffer from a number of internal contradictions that make its eventual self-destruction inevitable. Sooner or later, most of these arguments make an appearance in the writings of Christian thinkers who are opposed to capitalism.

CAPITALISM AND ECONOMIC CYCLES

Capitalism is thought to be irrational because it leads to drastic irregularities in economic cycles. Enemies of the free market object to it on grounds of its inherent tendency to produce boom-or-bust cycles. A market economy is supposed to be notoriously unstable.

> Even when it is performing at its best, capitalism is subject to booms and busts which take a frightful human toll in terms of insecurity and enforced idleness. At other times, as during the 1930's and to an increasing extent in the last few years, a condition of chronic stagnation and continuing mass unemployment is superimposed upon the normal ups and downs of the system.[1]

The market's alleged instability is used as grounds for justifying the need for the state to take over the reins of the economy.

1. Paul Sweezy. "Socialism and Communism as Ideals," *Monthly Review*, 1963, reprinted in *Up Against the American Myth*, op. cit., p. 417.

Murray Rothbard draws attention to the frequency with which the Great Depression is cited as proof of the instability of the free market.

> The chief impact of the Great Depression on American thought was universal acceptance of the view that '*laissez-faire* capitalism' was to blame. The common opinion—among economists and the lay public alike—holds that 'Unreconstructed Capitalism' prevailed during the 1920's and that the tragic depression shows that old-fashioned *laissez-faire* can work no longer. . . . The government must step in to stabilize the economy and iron out the business cycle. A vast army of people to this day consider capitalism almost permanently on trial. If the modern array of monetary-fiscal management and stabilizers cannot save capitalism from another severe depression, this large group will turn to socialism as the final answer.[2]

However, Rothbard counters, this common wisdom about the causes of the Great Depression must not be allowed to pass unchallenged. It rests, he insists, on the unproven "assumption that business cycles in general, and depressions in particular, arise from the depths of the free-market, capitalist economy." This assumption, he contends, "is pure myth, resting not on proof but on simple faith."[3] The truth is actually to be found in a competing economic tradition. As Rothbard explains, this competing "view holds that business cycles and depressions stem from disturbances generated in the market by *monetary intervention*. The monetary theory holds that money and credit expansion, launched by the banking system, causes booms and busts."[4] Interventionists love to claim that the Great Depression resulted from a basic flaw in capitalism and that only statist intervention adjusted the economy back to a

2. Rothbard, *America's Great Depression*, op. cit., p. 2. Rothbard appears to use "*laissez-faire*" in a broader sense than I did in an earlier chapter.
While important differences exist between Rothbard and Friedman, both accounts of the Great Depression are worth studying. See Milton and Rose Friedman, *Free to Choose* (New York: Harcourt, Brace, Jovanovich, 1980) pp. 74ff.
3. Ibid.
4. Ibid., p. 3.

stable position. Rothbard's book shows that the situation prior
to the Great Depression was anything but a period of unbridled
laissez-faire. The Depression resulted not from some defect
intrinsic to a market economy, but from government
mismanagement before, during, and after the economic collapse
of 1929. What made matters worse and turned what would have
been an otherwise moderate economic contraction (caused, of
course, by prior governmental mismanagement) into a major
disaster was an improper monetary policy adopted by the
Federal Reserve System between 1930-1931. Roosevelt's New
Deal was simply an example of additional intervention utilized
to prop up the failures of Herbert Hoover's earlier interventionist policies.

Periodic oscillations of prosperity and depression that critics
of the market believe are endemic to capitalism are, in fact, a
consequence of a fractional-reserve gold standard, especially one
that exists "with a central bank, a government and a public
opinion eager to keep expanding credit to start a 'full employment' boom or to keep it going. . . ."[5] As Henry Hazlitt explains,
business cycles are caused by monetary and credit expansion.

> The credit expansion does not raise all prices simultaneously and
> uniformly. Tempted by the deceptively low interest rates it
> initially brings about, the producers of capital goods borrow the
> money for new-long-term projects. This leads to distortions in
> the economy. It leads to overexpansion in the production of
> capital goods, and to other malinvestments that are only
> recognized as such after the boom has been going on for a
> considerable time. When this malinvestment does become
> evident, the boom collapses. The whole economy and structure
> of production must undergo a painful readjustment accompanied
> by greatly increased unemployment.[6]

Therefore, the reply of the free market to this critique is that
the kind of instability under discussion is not an inherent

5. Henry Hazlitt, "Gold Versus Fractional Reserves," *The Freeman*, 1979,
p. 264.
6. Ibid., pp. 264-265.

feature of the market. It results instead from governmental intervention with the market process that interrupts the market's informational function. For example, in a free market, low interest rates indicate that money is plentiful and that prospects for long range investment are favorable. High interest rates indicate a shortage of money and suggest the need for pessimism and caution. Interventionist policies that artificially alter the money supply and interest rates shut off this information. The major American depressions that occured in 1837, 1873, 1892, and 1929 were all

> . . . preceded by several years of government-inspired inflation of one kind or another. . . . There were other factors in these boom-and-bust cycles, but in each case the central ingredient has been credit expansion resulting from some form of government intervention. This is not to say that business fluctuations would not take place otherwise, for businessmen will often guess wrong, make mistakes, and will invest too deeply in the wrong place at the wrong time. But the effect will be local and short-lived. With the inexorable push of deliberate government policy, the entire economy usually finds itself swept along on a nation-wide wave of speculation that builds higher and higher and then collapses.[7]

Therefore, this particular attack on the market is a classic example of the market being blamed for the disastrous consequences of interventionist policies. The argument should actually be applied to economic interventionism.

CAPITALISM AND MONOPOLIES

The belief that capitalism leads inevitably to the establishment of monopolies is the basis for another claim that capitalism is irrational. In the view of those who advance this objection, capitalism is promoted on the premise that maximum competition will insure the perfect operation of the market whereas, in fact, the free market system encourages the

---

7. *The Incredible Bread Machine*, op. cit., pp. 32,33.

increased consolidation of power and capital into a few firms that gain effective monopolistic control. The very system that promotes competition leads to a destruction of competition. This kind of reasoning often assumes that larger firms gain such unfair advantage over smaller or less successful firms that prospective competitors find it impossible to gain effective access to the market while older and weaker competitors are driven out of business or absorbed in mergers. Once immunity from competition is attained, the argument continues, producers lose any incentive to produce the best products at the lowest price. Such domination of a market makes *de facto* price-fixing possible.

The monopolistic argument ignores evidence about how difficult it is to achieve actual control over a total market. While the Ralston Purina Company is perhaps the most successful company in the animal food market, it has been unable to extend that success into the human cereal market. Similarly, General Mills, an admittedly powerful force in the human cereal market, has been generally ineffectual in translating its manufacturing and marketing expertise into the animal food market.

Much of the plausibility of the monopolistic-argument depends upon a false picture of the market. It is surprising how many friends and enemies of the market persist in thinking that capitalism requires some kind of perfect competition. This model, a hangover from classical economics, is fallacious.

> Contrary to the way the market is defined by many, it is not the classical economic model where there are many sellers and many buyers. Rather . . . the market is simply what results from the free choices made by individuals without government interference. Indeed, the simple "many buyers/ many sellers" ideal is recognized by supporters of the market as static and without much choice or innovation while the market is actually dynamic and most complex and without any predetermined form.[8]

8. Donald Devine, *Does Freedom Work?* (Ottawa, Illinois: Caroline House Books, 1978) p. 44.

Textbook models of perfect competition often suggest a
"tendency for price to gravitate toward the equilibrium level
at which quantity demanded equals quantity supplied."[9] But
economists of the Austrian School like Von Mises, Hayek,
Kirzner, and Rothbard reject the *static* view of the market that
accompanies the notion of equilibrium. They offer instead a
dynamic model. For them, the market is constantly in a state
of process. Disequilibrium in the market "occurs precisely
because market participants do not know what the market-
clearing price is."[10] Because the defense of the free market does
not require any notion of perfect competition, the inability of
economists to discover such in the market counts as a mark
only against a faulty economic model and not against the
market itself. Static views of the market naturally encourage
a misguided pessimism about the market's tendency to
encourage the concentration of power and capital. In reality,
the market is a process of creative destruction with competing
forces attempting and often succeeding in wiping out the
opposition.

Abandonment of the static view of the market suggests still
another point overlooked by proponents of the monopolistic
argument. The dynamic view of the market "sees competition
as multiple and complex, where products compete on many
bases (price only being one) with all other products, actual and
potential."[11] In other words, even if one firm could, for a time,
gain dominance of the merchandising of a particular commodity,
it would still have to compete with the merchandisers of every
other commodity for the consumer's money. If people spend
their money on a new dress or suit, they no longer have that
money to spend for a theater ticket or a restaurant meal or a
new book or gasoline. The scarcity of commodities and money
forces the consumer to make an unending series of choices based
upon his particular valuations at the time. Once those choices

9. Kirzner, "Equilibrium," op. cit., p. 116.
10. Ibid.
11. Devine, op. cit., p. 52.

are made, that money is no longer available for other choices. In this kind of complex economic environment, no businessman can effectively control his customers. The car manufacturer is not simply competing against other car makers; he is competing with every other merchant of every other product; he is also competing with the tax collector. General Motors' present domination of the American automobile market won't mean a thing if enough consumers decide to forego the purchase of a new car for other commodities that they, at the time, value more highly.

It is widely believed that recent decades have seen an increase in the number of business failings as more and more power becomes concentrated in fewer companies. Donald Devine cites statistics that show how false this belief is. The evidence shows very little change in the rate of business failures.[12] Of course, Devine admits, plenty of evidence exists to show how political interference with the market (tariffs, regulations, subsidies, etc.) has the effect of offsetting market operations. But, he adds,

> . . . to the degree that the market is unfettered it appears that managers face restraints upon the wealth they nominally control. . . . If the market were as weak as critics suggest, it would seem that large corporations should at least be able to protect themselves from its forces. Yet there appears to be no positive correlation between concentration and lack of competition. Even some of the largest firms fail in the market. . . . When allowed to operate, though, the market buffets corporations and subjects them to its discipline. Even the most minimal theory of concentration—that a large corporation can hold its market position over time—does not stand up.[13]

The belief that capitalism breeds monopoly is contradicted by the evidence. The only real monopolies that have ever attained total immunity from competition achieved that status by governmental fiat, regulation, or support of some other kind.

12. Ibid.
13. Ibid., pp. 52-53. See Devine's book for statistical support for his claims. See also Yale Brozen, "The Antitrust Task Force Deconcentration Recommendation," *Journal of Law and Economics*, 1970, pp. 279-292.

Governments create monopolies by granting one organization the exclusive privilege of doing business or by establishing *de facto* monopolies through regulatory agencies whose alleged purpose is the enforcement of competition.[14] The only monopolies that pose a challenge to market principles are those that result from statist interference with the market.

CAPITALISM'S SUICIDAL TENDENCIES

According to this argument, capitalism is irrational because it contains within itself the seeds of its own destruction. This self-destruction is supposed to occur because capitalism leads to overproduction that makes economic disaster inevitable. William L. Baker summarizes this Marxist view:

> Capitalism, then, dies of gluttony. More correctly, capitalistic society dies of hunger induced by indigestion. . . . Production [under capitalism] was nothing other than a juggernaut relentlessly crushing everything in its path. Trade and prosperity were nothing else but the dormant seeds of a future crash. The only refuge from poverty (the effects of the crash) was to abstain from production and trade. In a word, the only refuge from poverty is poverty itself.[15]

Marx's analysis of the inevitable collapse of capitalism assumed that the capitalist's obsession with profit would lead him continually to expand production and reduce costs. His reduction of costs would entail paying his workers as little as possible. But the continued production would produce an oversupply of goods which the impoverished, victimized, and

14. See Friedman, *Capitalism and Freedom*, op. cit., chapters VIII-IX.
15. William L. Baker, "Marx and the Manifesto," *The Freeman*, 1979, pp. 681-2.

exploited workers would be unable to afford. Thus the capitalist's mad rush to profit will end in a glutted market. The fact that an insufficient number of consumers have the resources to afford his products is also his fault. Eventually, this house of cards must collapse.

Marx's "analysis" presumes an almost unbelievable stupidity on the part of the capitalist. If an employer has any sense at all, he will want to get the maximum productivity from his workers. If they are not paid enough to eat well and stay healthy, if they are not paid enough to remain motivated, the businessman deserves exactly what he will get. Even if a businessman lacks one grain of altruism, an enlightened self-interest should tell him that the well-being of his employees is important to his own survival. Marx also assumed that capitalists were incapable of learning from past mistakes of overproduction, that an incredible collection of errors would all be made at the same time, and that industrialists would persist in continuing production even when no one was able to purchase their products.

> How and why, with bulging inventories of unpurchased goods, would assembly belts continue to roll? Continued production under such circumstances would be suicidal and impossible. But capitalists are neither suicidal, overly charitable, nor infinitely rich. The Marxist sees the entrepreneur (or capitalist), however, as a total nitwit, completely unable to adapt to changing circumstances. And whatever else might be said of the industrialist magnate, he is not lacking in versatility. How could such a condition (overproduction) exist outside the realm of fairy tales and propaganda pamphlets? The law of scarcity has never been repealed. The issue of fallacies must be faced: the theory of overproduction is long overdue for a well-deserved rest.[16]

Once again, a frequently cited objection to the market appears plausible only because someone has stacked the deck. The myth of overproduction is a straw man.

16. Ibid., p. 683.

THE MYTH OF THE RATIONAL CONSUMER

Capitalism is judged irrational because of its erroneous assumption that consumers are rational creatures who will always seek the maximum satisfaction of their wants in a rational and predictable manner. But, this critic counters, consumers are notoriously irrational. They are frequently moved by habit, instinct, tradition or other non-rational influences to act in ways quite contrary to how a rational person in the market should behave. Consequently, the market is not the rational system its defenders believe it to be. For example, executives in the McDonald's organization might reasonably expect that their success in selling hamburgers in America and England can be easily repeated in any other country. This expectation would receive a rude shock, however, were they to attempt to sell hamburgers in Calcutta, India. Consumers do fail to behave in ways that someone obsessed by the rationality-thesis might expect. People often pay higher prices for products because of habit (they have always done business with a particular merchant) or convenience (the store is in their neighborhood) or some other reason. Consumers are notoriously fickle and unpredictable. If they were not, only businesses run by nitwits would ever fail.

Perhaps the most surprising thing about this argument is the fact that anyone seriously believes it applies to free market economics. The school of Austrian economics has sought for decades to counter models of the market that view it as an arena of rational satisfaction-maximizers. Austrian economists like Von Mises, Hayek, and Rothbard are correct in viewing *economic* value as purely subjective.[17] They are right in repudiating the notion that the economic value of anything is in some sense objective, that is, inherent in the object. Because the economic value people place upon things is completely subjective, it is impossible to predict what people will value, why

17. This view that economic value is subjective does not entail the subjectivity of other types of value such as moral value.

they will value it, and when their priorities might change. The economist can tell what people happen to value at the moment by their actions on the market. But past performance can never be a guarantee of future action. Consequently, this particular challenge to the free market rests, like many others, on a distorted model of how the market actually functions.

CAPITALISM AND UNEMPLOYMENT

Finally, capitalism is accused of being irrational because of its drastic inefficiencies that frequently result in high unemployment. John Maynard Keynes is supposed, by interventionist economists, to have shown the inefficiency of an unregulated market. As Arthur and Shaw explain, "Equilibrium[18] in a free-market system, can, in fact be reached at a less than optimal utilization of resources—at, for example a high rate of unemployment. Consequently, the market cannot be relied upon to eliminate poverty. Government intervention is necessary to accomplish this. . . ."[19] According to Bowie and Simon, who agree, the mechanism of the market can

. . . be stuck on a lower rung of the economic ladder. The ideal is to have equilibrium at or near full employment. However, Keynes showed that the self-regulating features of the market were not sufficient to guarantee equilibrium at this ideal position. The market can be in equilibrium at any level of employment.[20]

The argument commits several errors. One mistake, already noted, insists on applying the outmoded and false analogy of equilibrium to the free market. Attention has already been

18. The reader should notice the prominence given to the notion of equilibrium in the two quotations that summarize this objection to the market. We have already rejected the static model of the market that accompanies appeals to equilibrium.

19. Arthur, *Justice*, op. cit., p. 181.

20. Bowie, *The Individual*, op. cit., p. 194.

drawn to the distorted picture that results from this static model. The market is an on-going process that never approaches some kind of static equilibrium.

The argument is aided considerably by a false and misleading notion of what constitutes "full employment." Most often, this phrase is taken to mean a situation where everyone (or nearly everyone) has a job. This will never do. For one thing, the job market is a constantly changing process in which people continually enter and leave the job force. It is far more accurate to define "full employment" as a situation in which everyone who is willing and able to work at the prevailing wage rate is able to find a job. Suppose Mr. Jones announces that he will refuse any job that pays less than $50,000 a year. Should he be included in the unemployment statistics? Suppose Mr. Smith refuses any job that burns up more than 1000 calories in eight hours. Should he be counted? Under present statistical methods, both Jones and Smith would be counted as unemployed. Statistical number games such as this hinder a clear understanding of the unemployment picture.

The group of unemployed workers always includes four classes of people. (1) It includes new entrants to the job market such as high school graduates looking for their first full-time job. But if Miss Hale and Mr. Hearty declare themselves new entrants on June 1, why should they be immediately included within the ranks of the unemployed? (2) The second class of unemployed are those who have recently quit their old job. Their present unemployment is a result of their free choice. They could have remained employed, had they wished. Should their present lack of employment be laid at the door of the market system? (3) The third class would be those who have been recently fired. The job vacated because of their slothfulness or poor performance was immediately filled by someone else. (4) The final class of those without jobs are those who through no fault of their own were laid off as a result of their employer's declining business. There is good reason to regard this last class as the only group that should be counted as unemployed. The unemployment figures that are published each month include out-of-work breadwinners. But the statistics also include people seeking temporary work, people who are temporarily laid off who are receiving unemployment insurance, and people who are between jobs which are temporary such as substitute teachers. According to research done by the National Bureau of Economic Research, it is not at all unusual for less than half of those included in the unemployment statistics to be actually looking for work as their major activity.[21]

Comparatively few people remain unemployed for very long. The unemployment statistics suggest a picture of a huge army of victimized people totally unable to find work. The truth is that the statistics actually count people on their way to new employment, a situation which in three classes out of four, can hardly be blamed on the market. Why should the market be faulted for new entrants, re-entrants, and job-quitters? At any given time, the actual percentage of truly unemployed people among all those not working is a comparatively small percentage of the total. Even in the case of this last group, Rothbard notes, "Unemployment is caused by unions or government keeping wage rates above the free-market level."[22] When forces like unions and the state do not artificially raise wage rates higher than the current market, the market will do a remarkably effective job of providing employment for those willing to work at the market-rate. Of course, this claim will not satisfy the critic of the market because he will then retreat to other arguments already answered; that capitalists exploit the worker by paying unfairly low wages. This might be a good time to turn back to the beginning of the preceding chapter and read the following pages again.

CONCLUSION

The case against capitalism made on moral or rational

21. Robert E. Hall, *The Nature and Measurement of Unemployment*, National Bureau of Economic Research, Working Paper No. 252, July, 1978.
22. Rothbard, *Power and Market*, op. cit., p. 205.

grounds certainly appears less than overwhelming. What then accounts for the widespread and stubborn opposition to the system, even among those it has benefited the most? Perhaps more attention needs to be given to the *irrational* nature of much resistance to the market. Ernest van den Haag urges defenders of the market to "ask why their arguments have so little influence, why the policies they oppose continue, why the ideas they show to be wrong continue their hold on so many people. Ostrichlike, economists tend to ignore the nonrational sources of hostility to the market system."[23] It is sheer folly, he continues to attempt to "counter irrational ideologies with rational arguments . . . [and] act as though irrational pseudo-reasoning and chiliastic longings can be fought successfully by proper economic reasoning. . . . The attempt of economists to tutor the emotionally committed is as doomed to failure as the attempts of philosophers to tutor the insane."[24]

Several irrational prejudices probably underlie many attacks on the market. Kirzner suggests as one example, "resentments which can arise from frustrated ambitions, of the envy on the part of the intellectuals and the white collar workers of the good fortunes enjoyed by successful entrepreneurs."[25] Envy may also manifest itself as a suspicion on the part of the less fortunate classes that the unequal distribution of wealth must be due to some sinister activities on the part of the more fortunate.

James Burnham points to guilt as a likely affective state to explain the hostility of wealthy liberals to the free market.[26] The same suggestion has been made by the psychiatrist, Peter Breggin, himself a former liberal. Breggin has written candidly about how his own feelings of guilt played a role in his liberal commitment. He acknowledges, "I felt very guilty about my

23. Ernest Van Den Haag, *Capitalism: Sources of Hostility* (New Rochelle, New York: Epoch Books, 1979) p. 11.

24. Ibid., p. 12.

25. Kirzner, "The Ugly Market," op. cit., p. 733. Robert Nozick includes an excellent discussion of the role envy plays in opposition to the market. See his *Anarchy, State and Utopia*, op. cit., chapter 8.

26. James Burnam, *Suicide of the West* (New York: John Day, 1964).

advantages, and often thought about ways to help the disadvantaged classes."[27] Breggin goes on to say:

> The advantaged liberal idealist feels that his luck is unfair or unjust. In his heart he wishes everyone to have as much good luck or good fortune as he had. Extremists among advantaged liberal idealists are willing to sacrifice *all* of their good fortune even if it won't do anyone any good at all. Such an idealist is willing to sacrifice himself merely to "even the score" without advancing anyone's benefit. . . . To defend against his guilt, the advantaged liberal idealist develops the identity of "good guy with good intentions." He thinks of himself as someone who "means well." . . . This form of liberalism, as I lived it myself for many years, is not really a philosophy or a political ideology. It is a psychology of good intentions whose aim is not so much to bring about change in the outside world as it is to assuage guilt within the inner personal world.[28]

While others have suggested a possible role for guilt in attacks against the free market system, Breggin adds a somewhat novel twist.

> The righteousness of the advantaged liberal idealist smacks of religiosity, and indeed, the "liberalism" of this person comes much closer to religion than to politics: He seeks through his liberal humanitarianism to find redemption for the sin of being born with unfair advantage. Unlike the traditional Christian, his struggle is not with the temptation to enjoy sex, alcohol or secular philosophies. His temptation is to enjoy his undeserved advantages. But his struggle with this awful temptation is no less difficult than that of the religionist.[29]

It should be remembered that Breggin is a psychiatrist and former liberal who is first of all diagnosing his own former condition. He is then applying his new-found self-awareness to the cases of his former compatriots in the liberal cause. It is just possible that he has a point, even though it may not

27. Peter R. Breggin, "Libertarianism and the Liberal Ethos," *The Libertarian Review*, November 1979 (vol. 8) p. 31.
28. Ibid.
29. Ibid., p. 32.

correctly apply to every single liberal. But since evangelicals, perhaps better than most, should understand the extent to which human guilt can dominate the psyche and can lead to acts of rationalization in which an individual's true motives are obscurred, Breggin's analysis may deserve more careful attention.

Putting this suggestion aside and returning to the topic at hand, how strong is the case against capitalism? Not very, it would seem. And since the attack against capitalism on moral and rational grounds leaves so much to be desired, perhaps more attention should be given to the possibility that the real roots of much opposition to the market is non-rational in nature.

Chapter Twelve

Liberation Theology

One of the more influential movements to develop out of the contemporary Christian interest in justice is liberation theology. While liberation theology has taken a variety of forms that speak to the oppression of several types of different classes, the liberation theology in view in this chapter is the movement among Latin American Catholics and Protestants that seeks radical changes in the political and economic institutions of that region along Marxist lines. As one might expect, words like "conservative" and "capitalism" are labels applied to what liberation theologians perceive as the enemy—theories and institutions responsible for the oppression which liberation theologians oppose.

Most of the dialogue that liberation theologians have had with Americans to this point has been with liberals and socialists. It is extremely important that this dialogue be expanded to new fronts, namely, to frank and open discussions with representatives of the kind of conservativism represented by this book. But before this kind of dialogue can begin, some groundwork must be laid. For one thing, liberation theologians need to acquire greater precision in their use of the pivotal terms in the debate. Most books and articles written by liberation theologians assume that the reader understands what is meant by such key terms as "justice," "socialism," "Marxism," and "capitalism." Any reader who is unwilling to accept their use of the word "capitalism", for example, will obviously be unimpressed with their diagnosis of their society's ills, to say nothing about their prescription.

The investigation of liberation theology in this chapter will reduce the position to two basic theses. The *economic thesis* is the conviction of liberation theologians that capitalism is evil and socialism is good; the only hope for the poor and oppressed people of Latin America is for those nations to cast off the shackles of capitalism and embrace socialism. The *theological thesis* is a somewhat mixed bag of claims that reduces to the assertion that God is on the side of the poor and oppressed people of the world.

THE ECONOMIC THESIS

Juan Luis Segundo speaks for all liberation theologians when he writes that "one of the most urgent human problems facing the Latin American continent . . . [is] that of making a choice between capitalist society on the one hand or a socialist society on the other."[1] Few liberation theologians hesitate to call themselves Marxists. However, most of these Christian Marxists want it clearly understood that they do not equate their Marxism with that practiced by the state socialisms that dominate the Soviet-block countries. Archbishop Dom Helder Camera of Brazil has stated:

> I am a socialist. . . . But I don't see the solution in the socialist governments that exist today. . . . The Marxist record is awful. . . . God made man in his image and likeness, so he could become his co-creator and not a slave. . . . My socialism is a special one which respects the human person and turns to the gospel. My socialism is justice.[2]

In 1971, the Roman Catholic bishops of Peru urged Christians

1. "Capitalism Versus Socialism: Crux Theologica" in *Frontiers of Theology in Latin America*, ed. by Rosino Gibellini, tr. by John Drury (Maryknoll, New York: Orbis Books, 1979) p. 241.
2. Quoted in Miguez Bonino's book, *Doing Theology in a Revolutionary Situation* (Philadelphia: Fortress Press, 1975) p. 47. Note the Archbishop's last sentence, "My socialism is justice." It is an interesting but conveniently ambiguous slogan.

"to opt for socialism." Clarifying this proposal, however, they went on to say: "We do not mean a bureaucratic, totalitarian, or atheistic socialism; we mean a socialism that is both humanistic and Christian."[3]

Liberation theologians usually insist that the so-called orthodox Marxism represented by Soviet-brand communism is a heresy, unsupported by a careful study of the full corpus of Marx's writings. A good example of the Marxist revisionism practiced by many liberation theologians is Jose Miranda's book, *Marx Against the Marxists*,[4] a title that suggests the extent to which thinkers like Miranda will go in their attempt to rescue "the real Marx" from the distortions that decades of misinterpretation and ideological mishandling have introduced into his thought. Miranda offers scores of passages from Marx's own writings which he believes contradict the official Marxist reading of Marx. Miranda believes that the Marxist orthodoxy that emanates from Soviet-controlled nations has falsified Marx's message. Miranda's Marx is not a materialistic and atheistic economic determinist. He is instead a man with high moral ideals whose commitment to humanitarian goals was so sincere and so uncompromising that Miranda feels no hesitation in regarding Marx as a Christian. In fact, Miranda's book carries the arresting subtitle, "The Christian Humanism of Karl Marx." Just a few quotations from Miranda's book will indicate how far he is willing to go in his revision of Marx and, some might add, in his total recasting of Christian theology:

> The Christianity of an author does not consist exclusively in his or her affirmation of the existence of God. If the whole doctrine of an author is aimed at provoking a very specific kind of revolution in the world, then the specific motive of this revolution is an incomparable indication as to whether the author's thinking is Christian or not.[5]

Similarly if Marx's fundamental and thoroughgoing criticism of

---

3. Enrique Dussel, *History and the Theology of Liberation*, tr. by John Drury (Maryknoll, New York: Orbis Books, 1976) p. 134.
4. (Maryknoll, New York: Orbis Books, 1980).
5. Ibid., p. xi.

capitalism centers around the fact that capitalism does not respect human beings as persons, as real subjects and agents, then that analysis turns out to be eminently Christian. . . . And that is far more substantial and important than explicit professions of faith.[6]

Miranda's strenous efforts to show that the later Marx was really a Christian is an indication of the extent to which liberation theologians will go in their attempt to make Marxist revolutionary activity respectable in the eyes of the Christian church.

A growing number of American evangelicals share the liberation theologian's contempt for what they call "capitalism" and their infatuation with Marxism. One evangelical who can hardly restrain his enthusiasm for Marxism is Jim Wallis, editor of the journal, *Sojourners*. Wallis writes longingly of the day when "more Christians will come to view the world through Marxist eyes. . . ." He thinks that day is inevitable. It will, he writes, "even be predictable among the so-called 'young evangelicals' who, for the most part, have a zeal for social change that is not yet matched by a developed socio-economic analysis that will cause them to see the impossibility of making capitalism work for justice and peace." Wallis thinks there are several factors that make the recent Christian alliance with Marxism understandable. These include "an acute sense of political injustice, a sharpened social analysis which perceives the essential corruption of the present system, and a compassion for those who suffer from the existing order of things."[7] It should be noted that Wallis' "sharpened social analysis" and "developed socio-economic analysis" is unavoidably tied to the misrepresentations of capitalism and the faulty objections to the market system critiqued in earlier chapters. The foundation for the Christian Marxism that he recommends looks to be about as solid as quicksand.

6. Ibid.
7. Jim Wallis, "Liberation and Conformity," *Mission Trends No. 4, Liberation Theologies in North America and Europe* (Grand Rapids: Eerdmans, 1979) pp. 54-55.

Less radical liberation theologians and evangelicals who accept the general position advanced by this book can agree on a number of significant points. (1) First, they can agree that the plight of the poor in Latin America is desperate enough to warrant drastic action. Earlier in this book, we wrote:

> Economic freedom is a necessary condition for personal and political liberty. No one can be free in the political sense if he lacks economic freedom. Economic freedom aids the existence and growth of political liberty by helping to check the concentration of too much power in the hands of too few people. As long as a large percentage of the people in a society exercise ownership control, power within that society will be more widely diffused. No one can be free when he is dependent upon others for the basic economic needs of life. If someone commands what a person can or cannot buy and sell, then a significant part of that individual's freedom has been abridged. Human beings who are dependent upon any one power for the basic essentials of life are not free. When that master becomes the state, obedience becomes a prerequisite to employment and to life itself.

In the context of chapter 7, those words were an apology for the economic freedom of capitalism. In the context of liberation theology, those very same words can serve as an indictment of those in Latin American countries who persist in denying economic freedom to the masses. There is no reason why the evangelical conservative and the liberation theologian have to disagree about objectives. One persistent and puzzling question is why the oppressive establishments of Latin American countries that oppose genuine economic freedom should be referred to as capitalist.

(2) The conservative evangelical and the liberation theologian can also agree in their opposition to the totalitarian socialism practiced by the state socialisms of the world and to the brand of Marxism regarded as orthodox by the leaders of these states.

(3) They can also agree in their rejection of the essentially interventionist nature of the dominant economies of the Western nations. The basic mistake liberation theologians make again is thinking that this economic interventionism is identical with

capitalism. It is not. Once this mistaken identification is made, it is a simple matter to blame capitalism for all of the unfortunate economic consequences that thinkers like Von Mises predicted whenever the state interferes with the operations of the market. But this blame is misdirected.

Where do the evangelical conservative and the liberation theologian disagree? They certainly disagree in their assessment of socialism. As our earlier analysis of socialism revealed, it is no accident that state socialism results in a dehumanizing totalitarianism. Nor should we be impressed by appeals to an unattainable non-statist socialist utopia. The arguments why every attempt at a socialist economy must fail have already been noted.

The political conservative and liberation theologian will probably continue to disagree in their analysis of and assessment of capitalism. This is especially unfortunate. No workable economy is feasible that does not take account of the operations of the market, as they have been described in earlier chapters. Any economy that violates those principles is doomed to failure and, even worse, bound to create conditions in which human liberation becomes less attainable.

Walter Benjamin wonders why so many liberation theologians focus their attention exclusively on Latin America and "are all but mute on totalitarianism in Eastern Europe."[8] After all, he points out, people in Eastern Europe are also oppressed and poor but no one ever says a word on their behalf. "Whatever the reason, the near silence of liberation theology regarding Eastern Europe reveals ethical astigmatism."[9] Benjamin's censure of its exclusive preoccupation with oppression in Latin America is an important mark against liberation theology. People who profess concern about justice and freedom should condemn bondage wherever it exists including the Marxist states of the world. Ironically, Benjamin points out, there is

8. Walter W. Benjamin, "Liberation Theology: European Hopelessness Exposes the Latin Hoax," *Christianity Today*, vol. 26, March 5, 1982, p. 21.
9. Ibid.

also a modest revolution beginning in Eastern Europe; but it is a revolution *against* Marxism. "Liberationists should be more ecumenical in their humanistic sympathy. Too often, victims of Soviet oppression and their Eastern satraps, Boat People, Afghan rebels, the Kurds and Bahaists of Iran, Cuban political prisoners and exiles, and black victims of black dictators in Africa are ignored because the choice of underdog is selective and rooted in ideological criteria. Some liberation theologians . . . cannot admit injustice or oppression in Vietnam because, by definition, socialist countries cannot oppress."[10]

In this connection, it is interesting to see how often Christian journals like *Sojourners* expose and denounce oppression in Marxist states. The fact is that such criticism is seldom if ever given. Christians sympathetic to Marxism too often ignore or cover over the deficiencies and failures of socialist revolutions. Benjamin makes one more point worth noting: "Liberation theology should give up the penchant to believe the worst about the United States. It is a mystery to me why some liberationists who prize an autonomous lifestyle are so enamored by masses of people in motion in closed societies . . . "[11] Liberation theologians need to consider the possibility that a capitalism not yet tried in Latin America may be the best hope for the poor and oppressed people in that region.

THE THEOLOGICAL THESIS

One recent essay that serves admirably as a fair summary of liberation theology is authored by Ronald J. Sider, whose sympathy with the movement is obvious from his many writings in the area of social philosophy.[12] Sider sums up the

10. Ibid., p. 22.
11. Ibid., p. 23.
12. See, for example, Sider's *Rich Christians in an Age of Hunger*. op. cit. My remarks are based on his essay, "An Evangelical Theology of Liberation," from *Perspectives on Evangelical Theology*, edited by Kenneth Kantzer and Stanley Gundry (Grand Rapids: Baker, 1980) pp. 117-133.

theological thesis of liberation theology by writing: "God is on the side of the poor and oppressed." (p. 117) This certainly has a nice ring to it. Most people like to pull for the underdog. Sider tells us that God is on the side of all of the world's underdogs. As inspiring as Sider's thesis is, it has one obvious fault: it has no clear meaning. We can shout that God is on the side of the poor all we want. Sooner or later, someone is going to want to know what this slogan means; and that is where the problems begin.

To his credit, Sider recognizes how ambiguous the theological thesis is. Even more praiseworthy, Sider realizes that several of the most commonly given explications of the thesis are either false or heretical. He identifies and criticizes a number of these erroneous interpretations.

First of all, Sider warns that it is wrong to interpret the theological thesis ("God is on the side of the poor and the oppressed") to mean that the Bible encourages people to actively seek a life of material poverty. This is so obvious as to require no further comment.

Secondly, Sider writes," I do not mean that the poor and oppressed are, because they are poor and oppressed, to be idealized or automatically included in the church." (pp. 117-118) He thinks some liberation theologians have blurred the distinction between the company of redeemed believers and the world. The poor, Sider insists, are not saved simply because they are poor. "The poor sinfully disobey God in the same way that we wretched middle-class sinners do and they therefore need to enter into a living personal relationship with Jesus Christ. Only then do they become a part of the church." (p. 118) Sider's reply could not have been put any better.

The third incorrect interpretation of the theological thesis that Sider notes is "that God cares more about the salvation of the poor than the salvation of the rich or that the poor have a special claim on the gospel." (p. 118) One liberation theologian who has actually stated this unbiblical view is Enco Gatti: "The human areas that are poorest in every way are the most qualified for receiving the Saving Word. They are the ones that have the best right to that Word; they are the privileged recipients of the Gospel."[13] Sider correctly counters this aberrant view by noting that God's love for a human being is neither increased nor lessened as a result of that person's wealth. It is false to say "that God desires the salvation of the poor more than the salvation of the rich." (p. 119)

Another erroneous interpretation of the theological thesis is the belief "that knowing God is nothing more than seeking justice for the poor and oppressed." (p. 119) Regrettably, this unbiblical position has been advanced by a few liberation theologians. Jose Miranda, for one, has maintained, "To know Yahweh is to achieve justice for the poor."[14] Sider expresses regret for Miranda's simplistic radicalism because it gives all liberation theology a bad name.

Up to this point in his essay, Sider has done a good job of telling his reader what the theological thesis of liberation theology should not be taken to mean. Unfortunately, by the time Sider has made all of the qualifications and exclusions required to save his thesis from nonsense or heresy, he has little positive content left. Sider has told us what it does *not* mean to say is that God is in the side of the poor, and done a fine job in the process. But what in his view *is* the meaning of the thesis? At this point, Sider's gift for clarity and organization seems to leave him. He states that his own interpretation of the theological thesis will be developed in terms of three points:

1. At the central points of revelation history, God also acted to liberate the poor and oppressed.
2. God acts in history to exalt the poor and oppressed and to cast down the rich and oppressive.
3. God's people, if they are truly God's people, are also on the side of the poor and oppressed. (p. 120)

As best as can be determined, Sider seems to think these three

13. *Rich Church-Poor Church* (Maryknoll: Orbis Books, 1974) p. 43.
14. Jose Miranda, *Marx and the Bible* (Maryknoll: Orbis Books, 1974) p. 44.

claims taken together will explain what it does mean to say that God is on the side of the poor and oppressed. It is important therefore to see how Sider develops and supports these three points.

Sider's first point could be called *The Exodus Thesis* since it is the historic and miraculous deliverance of Israel from Egypt that is most often cited as a demonstration of God's activity on behalf of the poor and oppressed. As Sider puts it, "At the central moments when God displayed his mighty acts in history to reveal his nature and will [like the exodus], God also intervened to liberate the poor and oppressed." (p. 120) One has to be very careful with this kind of argument lest things go too far in the wrong direction. It is probably true that all of the Israelites delivered in the exodus were oppressed human beings. Most slaves are. It is also likely that the Jews enslaved in Egypt were poor. Few of us have met many wealthy slaves. We ought therefore to be suspicious about any argument that runs as follows: because all of the Jews whom God delivered from Egypt were poor and oppressed slaves, it follows that God's only reason for delivering them was their poverty and oppressed state. God had reasons for the exodus that transcend the fact that the Israelites were poor and oppressed. To Sider's credit, he does take a moment to criticize any who would view the exodus *exclusively* in terms of God's delivering people from poverty and oppression. He writes, "God acted at the exodus to call a special people so that through them he could reveal his will and bring salvation to all people." (p. 121) Sider is certainly correct. But why then should the poverty and oppression of the Israelites not be viewed as an essentially accidental feature of the exodus? The clear fact that God's primary concern in the exodus and His other mighty acts was with some other end (such as the deliverance of human beings from sin) makes incidental or irrelevant the accompanying fact that the people God delivered contained large numbers of the poor. Any claim that God's primary reason for acting in these cases was the poverty of the people involves a serious misordering of God's priorities. It is difficult therefore to see much value in Sider's first point.

In explaining the second point used to elaborate the claim that God is on the side of the poor, Sider writes: "God acts in history to exalt the poor and to cast down the rich and oppressive." (p. 120) It is obvious that this statement is a claim about something that Sider believes has happened in history. Anyone unfamiliar with his essay might assume that since he has made an empirical claim about something that has happened repeatedly in history, Sider will follow up that claim with a recitation of the historical evidence that supports his assertion. But such is not the case. Sider's discussion of his historical claim fails to provide one single shred of historical evidence. Instead, he takes his reader on a quick journey through the Bible as he cites various proof-texts that supposedly support his point. This is a remarkable procedure for a historian who is attempting to support a claim about history. Suppose a different writer had claimed, for example, that God acts in history to exalt the United States and to cast down its enemies. An assertion like this ought to be supported with fairly substantial amounts of historical evidence. But suppose the proponent of the thesis that God acts in history to exalt the United States does not even attempt to provide historical evidence for his claim but offers instead assorted proof-texts from the Bible. Would we not find such a procedure odd, to say the least? And yet this is exactly how Sider attempts to support his thesis that God acts in history to exalt the poor.

Up to this point, Sider has identified the basic thesis of liberation theology as the belief that God is on the side of the poor and oppressed. But the thesis is ambiguous. What does it *mean* to say that God is on the side of the poor and oppressed? Sider correctly excludes a number of false or dangerous interpretations of the thesis. But when it comes time for him to state what the thesis does mean, he does so in terms of three additional points. His first two points did not advance the understanding of the theological thesis one step. The first point, that God's mighty acts like the exodus were acts to liberate the poor, is based on a fallacy. It takes the fact that many whom God delivered were poor and elevates their poverty into the primary reason for His acting. Nor did Sider's second point fare much better. There, we found, he made a historical claim which not only seems contradicted by the evidence (the company of the poor is not growing smaller as God acts on their behalf) but is left totally unsupported by the kind of historical evidence that such a claim requires.

Therefore all that remains of Sider's attempt to explicate the meaning of the theological thesis is his third point which he explains as follows: "God's people, if they are truly God's people, are also on the side of the poor and oppressed." Several things should be noted here. To this point, Sider has failed to tell his reader what it means to say that *God* is on the side of the poor and oppressed. But now he attempts to explain that thesis by saying that *God's people* should be on the side of the poor and oppressed. If we don't know what it means for God to be on the side of the poor, we certainly won't know what it means for God's people to be on their side. Sider has explained one unknown with another unknown. It is one thing to care enough about the poor to want to be on their side. It is something else to discover the best and most lasting means to help them.

From its first chapter, this book has sought to make a distinction between ends and means. Biblically informed Christians participating in the debates we have described should have a consensus, however general, about the ends they think are best. The disagreements among conservatives, liberals, socialists and so-called Christian Marxists are largely differences over the best means to reach those ends. Sider thinks the essence of liberation theology can be expressed in the empty formula, God is on the side of the poor and oppressed. Until the formula is given some meaningful content, it is something any believer can accept. Every believer can also agree that he or she had better be on the side of the poor and oppressed. But the central question concerns how this support and concern for the poor should be translated into practice.

It should be obvious that there is plenty of room for disagreement as to how one's being on the side of the poor will manifest itself. Genuine Christian commitment involves concern for and action on behalf of the needy and oppressed. The claim is probably so obvious that Sider's elaborate attempts to provide proof are superfluous. The really crucial question deals with how that concern should be expressed. Is it possible that one real enemy of the poor in the United States is the liberal welfare state? Is it possible that attempts to replace the present oppressive institutions of Latin America with an ill-formed utopian socialist ideal could only serve to prolong the misery of the masses?

It would be a mistake to think that political conservatives have to oppose all liberation theology. But conservatives will insist that socialist attempts to liberate people will fail. What the countries of Latin America need is a *new* liberation theology. One of the ways in which a new liberation theology would differ from the old is in its more realistic assessment of the inescapable failure of all utopian socialist schemes and its more careful distinction between capitalism and the forms of economic interventionism which are the real culprits that liberation theology intends to condemn. The only way in which the poor of any nation can be delivered economically from their poverty is through an economic system that first of all produces enough wealth so that all are capable of sharing. Economic systems that decrease or discourage production can never succeed in eliminating poverty; they can only make it worse. It is time to consider the outlines of a new liberation theology that will recognize the fundamental role of free markets in any economic system.

James Skillen, summarizing what he understands as the fundamental concern of moderate liberation theologians, states the belief "that God is calling human beings to create *new* social, economic, and political structures that will free men rather than keep them enslaved."[15] This goal is far more compatible with the vision of capitalism given in this book than with any kind of socialism that is attainable in the real world. The first prerequisite of any sound social theory has to be a realistic analysis and assessment of the weaknesses and possibilities of the human beings who exist on this planet. Quite frankly, realism is the last thing liberation theology has going for it.

15. James Skillen, "History and the Unfolding of Society," *Pro Rege*, June, 1981, p. 10.

Acknowledgments

Grateful acknowledgment is given to the University Press of America for its permission to use some material from my earlier book, *Freedom, Justice and the State*. I also appreciate permission from the editors of *The Intercollegiate Review* and *Christianity Today* to include material from some of my articles previously published in their journals. The articles are cited below. Special acknowledgment is made to the following publishers for their permission to quote:

From *Capitalism and Freedom* by Milton Friedman by permission of The University of Chicago Press, Copyright 1962.

From *Capitalism and the Historians*, edited by Friedrich A. Hayek by permission of The University of Chicago Press. Copyright 1954.

From *Law, Legislation and Liberty*, Vol. II: *The Mirage of Social Justice* by Friedrich A. Hayek by permission of The University of Chicago Press. Copyright 1976.

From *Law, Legislation and Liberty*, Vol. III: *The Political Order of a Free People* by Friedrich A. Hayek by permission of The University of Chicago Press. Copyright 1979.

From *Ethics*, "Liberty Without Fraternity," by B. J. Diggs (Volume 87, January, 1977) by permission of The University of Chicago Press.

From *Ethics*, "Welfare and Freedom," by Norman E. Bowie (Volume 89, April 1979) by permission of The University of Chicago Press.

Bibliography

Arthur, John and Shaw, William H., editors. *Justice and Economic Distribution* (Englewood Cliffs, New Jersey: Prentice-Hall, 1978)

Barry, Brian. *The Liberal Theory of Justice* (New York: Oxford University Press, 1973).

Banfield, Edward. *The Unheavenly City* (Boston: Little, Brown & Co., 1968).

Beckman, David M. *Where Faith And Economics Meet* (Minneapolis: Augsburg, 1981).

Bedau, Hugo, editor, *Justice and Equality* (Englewood Cliffs, New Jersey: Prentice-Hall, 1971).

Beichman, A., Martino, A. and Minogue, K. *Three Myths* (Washington, D.C.: The Heritage Foundation, 1982).

Bell, Daniel and Kristol, Irving. *The Crisis in Economic Theory* (New York: Basic Books, 1981).

Benjamin, Walter W. "Liberation Theology: European Hopelessness Exposes the Latin Hoax." *Christianity Today*, March 5, 1982.

Bockmuehl, Klaus. *The Challenge of Marxism* (Downers Grove: Intervarsity Press, 1980).

Bonino, Miguez. *Doing Theology in a Revolutionary Situation* (Philadelphia: Fortress Press, 1975).

Bowie, Norman E. and Simon, Robert L., editors. *The Individual and the Political Order* (Englewood Cliffs, New Jersey: Prentice-Hall, 1977).

Bowie, Norman E. "Welfare and Freedom," *Ethics*, Vol. 89 (1979).

Brown, Susan Love, et al. *The Incredible Bread Machine* (San Diego: World Research, Inc., 1974).

Brozen, Yale. "Is Government the Source of Monopoly?" *The Intercollegiate Review*, Vol. 5 (1968-69).

Chilton, David. *Productive Christians in an Age of Guilt Manipulators* (Tyler, Texas: Institute for Christian Economics, 1981).

Cullmann, Oscar. *The State in the New Testament* (New York: Charles Scribner's Sons, 1956).

DeGeorge, Richard T. and Picheler, Joseph A., editors. *Ethics, Free Enterprise and Public Policy* (New York: Oxford University Press, 1978).

Dengerink, Ja. *The Idea of Justice in Christian Perspective* (Toronto: Wedge, 1978).

Dussel, Enrique. *History and the Theology of Liberation.* tr. John Drury (Maryknoll, New York: Orbis, 1980).

Evans, M. Stanton. *Clear and Present Dangers* (New York: Harcourt Brace Jovanovich, 1975).

Feinberg, Joel and Gross, Hyman, editors. *Justice: Selected Readings* (Encino, California: Dickenson Publishing Co., 1977).

Feinberg, Joel. *Social Philosophy* (Englewood Cliffs, New Jersey: Prentice-Hall, 1973).

Friedman, Milton. *Capitalism and Freedom* (Chicago: University of Chicago Press, 1962).

Friedrich, C. J. and Chapman, J., editors. *Justice* (New York: Aldine-Atherton, 1963).

Frykenberg, Robert. "World Hunger: Food is not the Answer." *Christianity Today.* December 11, 1981.

Gatti, Enco. *Rich Church—Poor Church* (Maryknoll, New York: Orbis, 1974).

Gibellini, Rosino, editor. *Frontiers of Theology in Latin America.* tr. John Drury. (Maryknoll, New York: Orbis, 1979).

Gilder, George. *Wealth and Poverty* (New York: Basic Books, 1981).

Grounds, Vernon. *Evangelicalism and Social Responsibility* (Scottsdale, Pa.: Herald Press, 1969).

Hayek, Friedrich, editor. *Capitalism and the Historians* (Chicago: University of Chicago Press, 1954).

Hayek, Friedrich. *The Constitution of Liberty* (Chicago: University of Chicago Press, 1960).

Hayek, Friedrich. *Law, Legislation and Liberty*, 3 volumes (Chicago: University of Chicago Press, 1973-1979).

Hayek, Friedrich. *The Road to Serfdom* (Chicago: University of Chicago Press, 1944).

Hazlitt, Henry. *The Conquest of Poverty* (New Rochelle: Arlington House, 1973).

Hazlitt, Henry. *The Inflation Crisis and How to Solve it* (New Rochelle: Arlington House, 1978).

Hazlitt, Henry. "Understanding 'Austrian' Economics," *The Freeman*, Feb. 1981.

Held, Virginia, editor. *Property, Profits and Economic Justice* (Belmont, California: Wadsworth, 1980).

Hobbs, Charles D. *The Welfare Industry* (Washington: The Heritage Foundation, 1978).

Hospers, John. *Libertarianism* (Los Angeles: Nash Publishing Co., 1971).

Kelbley, Charles A. *The Value of Justice* (New York: Fordham University Press, 1979).

Kirzner, Israel. "The Ugly Market: Why Capitalism is Hated, Feared and Despised." *The Freeman.* Volume 24 (1974).

Leiser, Burton M. *Liberty, Justice and Morals* (New York: Macmillan, 2nd edition, 1979).

Johnston, Robert K. *Evangelicals at an Impasse* (Atlanta: John Knox Press, 1979).

Lucas, J. R. *On Justice* (Oxford: Charendon Press, 1980).

Machan, Tibor, editor. *The Libertarian Alternative* (Chicago: Nelson-Hall, 1974).

Mavrodes, George. "On Helping the Hungry." *Christianity Today.* Dec. 30, 1977.

Meyer, Frank. *In Defense of Freedom* (Chicago: Henry Regnery, 1962).

Miranda, Jose. *Marx and the Bible* (Maryknoll, New York: Orbis, 1974).

Mott, Stephen Charles. *Biblical Ethics and Social Change* (New York: Oxford University Press, 1982).

Nash, Ronald. *Freedom, Justice and the State* (Washington: University Press of America, 1980).

Nock, Albert Jay. *Our Enemy, the State* (New York: Arno Press, 1972).

Novak, Michael, editor. *The Denigration of Capitalism* (Washington: American Enterprise Institute, 1979).

Nozick, Robert. *Anarchy, State and Utopia* (New York: Basic Books, 1974).

Oppenheimer, Franz. *The State* (New York: Vanguard Press, 1926).

Pasour, E. C. Jr. "On Economic Justice," *Modern Age*, 1981.

Perelman, Chaim. *Justice* (New York: Random House, 1967).

Petuchowski, Jacob J. "The Altar Throne Clash Updated." *Christianity Today.* Sept. 23, 1977.

Rasmussen, Larry L. *Economic Anxiety and Christian Faith* (Minneapolis: Augsburg, 1981).

Rawls, John. *A Theory of Justice* (Cambridge: Harvard University Press, 1971).

Reisman, George. *The Government Against the Economy* (Ottawa, Illinois: Caroline House, 1979).

Rogge, Benjamin. "Christian Economics: Myth or Reality?" *The Freeman.* Dec., 1965.

Ropke, Wilhelm *A Humane Economy* (Chicago: Henry Regnery Co., 1960).

Rose, Tom and Metcalf, Robert. *The Coming Victory* (Memphis: Christian Studies Center, 1980).

Rothbard, Murray N. *America's Great Depression* (Kansas City: Sheed and Ward, 1975).

Rothbard, Murray N. *For a New Liberty* (New York: Macmillan, 1978 revised edition).

Schaeffer, David Lewis. *Justice or Tyranny? A Critique of John Rawls' Theory of Justice* (Port Washington, N.Y.: Kennikat Press, 1979).

Sider, Ronald. "An Evangelical Theology of Liberation." in *Perspectives on Evangelical Theology*, edited by Kenneth Kantzer and Stanley Gundry (Grand Rapids: Baker, 1979).

Sider, Ronald. *Rich Christians in an Age of Hunger* (Downers Grove, Illinois: Intervarsity Press, 1977).

Sowell, Thomas. *Ethnic America, A History* (New York: Basic Books, 1981).

Sowell, Thomas. *Markets and Minorities* (New York: Basic Books. 1981).

Sowell, Thomas. *Race and Economics* (New York: David McKay, 1975).

Sowell, Thomas. "The Uses of Government for Racial Equality." *National Review.* Sept. 4, 1981.

Spadaro, Louis M. *New Directions in Austrian Economics* (Kansas City: Sheed, Andrews and McMeel, 1978).

Sterba, James. *Justice: Alternative Political Perspectives* (Belmont: Wadsworth, 1980).

Templeton, Kenneth S., editor. *The Politicization of Society* Indianapolis: Liberty Press, 1979).

Van Den Haag, Ernest, editor. *Capitalism: Sources of Hostility* (New Rochelle: Epoch Books, 1979).

Vickers, Douglas. *Economics and Man* (Philadelphia: The Craig Press, 1976).

Wallis, Jim. "Liberation and Conformity" in *Mission Trends No. 4, Liberation Theologies in North American and Europe* (Grand Rapids: Eerdmans, 1979).

Ward, Benjamin. *The Ideal Worlds of Economics* (New York: Basic Books, 1979).

Wogaman, J. Philip. *The Great Economic Debate: An Ethical Analysis* (Philadelphia: The Westminster Press, 1977).

DATE L